FAST FRENCH

FAST FRENCH

100 Recipes for Stylish Dishes in Minutes

MARIE-PIERRE MOINE

Photography by
DAVID GILL

CONRAN OCTOPUS

For my sister Anne-Sophie Naudin. *Vite fait, bien fait.*

First published in 1993 by
Conran Octopus Limited
37 Shelton Street,
London WC2H 9HN

Text copyright © 1993 Marie-Pierre Moine
Photography copyright © 1993 David Gill
Design and layout copyright © 1993 Conran Octopus Limited

Both metric and imperial quantities are given in the recipes
in this book. Use either all metric or all imperial,
as the two are not necessarily interchangeable.

Editorial Direction **Lewis Esson Publishing**
Art Direction **Karen Bowen**
Painted backgrounds **Lynne Robinson and Richard Lowther**
Editorial Assistant **Penny David**
Food for Photography **Meg Jansz**
Styling **Róisín Nield**
Production **Alison McIver**

Cataloging-in-Publication Data: a catalogue record for this book
is available from the British Library

ISBN 1 85029 513 1

Typeset by Hunters Armley Limited
Printed in China

CONTENTS

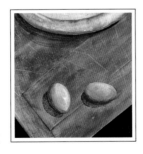

ACKNOWLEDGEMENTS 128

INTRODUCTION

French food, with its tempting sautés, scrumptious salads, colourful snacks and exquisite ways with vegetables, allows a wide range of deliciously surprising dishes to be cooked in minutes.

From *moules marinière* to *sole meunière, côtes de porc* and *frisée aux lardons*, a lot of the appetizing dishes one associates with the home cooking of France may be made very comfortably in around 30 minutes from scratch to finish. More often than not this only involves 10 to 15 minutes of concentrated activity. This was my first pleasant discovery when I began to get involved in this book. Then as I went along, I began to work on ways of simplifying other classic recipes and techniques without sacrificing the taste and style of the end result – the finished dish. Later on, I felt ready to create my own Fast French dishes.

Several were inspired by memorable eating experiences I had enjoyed somewhere or other in France. The best *mouclade* (page 71) I ever had was in a wind-swept beach-hut café on a dreary stretch of coast not far from Les Sables d'Olonne. The place was damp and unprepossessing, but we were hungry and miles from anywhere. We sat there gloomily waiting for the *plat du jour* with a glass of throat-corroding Gros Plant. Suddenly there was a glorious smell and a great steaming platter was put in front of us . . . *mouclade*. I never asked for the recipe but the combination of juicy mussels and mellow faintly spiced 'soup' was very much in my mind when I worked on my version of the dish.

Brochettes de Fruits Caramelisées (page 118) and Poires au Roquefort (page 114) were both inspired by enjoyable meals I had in Brive, South-West France. The pear I remember particularly fondly. It was put in front of me, perfect and red-glazed, proudly standing in the centre of an immaculate plate. It was chilled and filled with a creamy Roquefort mixture. My companion and I agreed that the presentation was a clever idea and got carried away into gourmet musings. Perhaps the combination of flavours would taste better at room temperature or even *tiède?* And what about also serving fresh walnuts and black chocolate truffles? My pears with blue cheese sauce are very prosaic by comparison but they are a good grown-up pudding for people who don't have a sweet tooth.

THE FAST FRENCH APPROACH

The recipes in this book are written for enthusiast amateurs by another enthusiastic home cook: there is nothing complicated, stuffy or pretentious about *Fast French*. Fast cooking has its limitations, the most important being that you have to use top quality fresh ingredients since there is little time for radical improvements on what is there in the first place. Understand the limitations and make the most of the possibilities – vibrant flavours, strong textures and fresh appeal. Don't be over ambitious but have all your equipment and ingredients ready before you start and set to work wholeheartedly. One of the joys of fast cooking is that you can savour the fruit of your labour almost immediately: you'll be sitting down to a proper French meal very shortly.

While the book generally follows the time-honoured order of the traditional French *repas*, from *hors d'œuvre* to *fromages, fruits et desserts,* it acknowledges the increasing popularity of lighter meals with a chapter on snacks. In France, as elsewhere, eating habits are changing, slowly perhaps but noticeably. It must be said, however, that French people are not great 'snackers'. The idea behind *un petit snack* is a quick light collation, a mini-meal consumed instead of a proper meal, not as the basis of a standard regular daily diet.

Menu suggestions for meals *à la française* to suit different occasions are given on page 126.

EQUIPMENT

Until the last few years, the French domestic kitchen was a pretty basic place as far as equipment was concerned. Even in the most elegant apartment it tended to be a poky dark room tucked away at the back, often overlooking an inner courtyard and rows of dustbins. People made do with a gas cooker, a few trusted pots and pans, a chopping board and a couple of knives. It took a long time for electricity to replace elbow grease. I was brought up watching mayonnaise being beaten with a wooden spoon and vegetables shredded in a manual *mouli*.

These days I have found room in my miniscule kitchen for a Magimix, a hand-held electric whisk, a much-loved compact dishwasher and a few other gadgets, but deep down I am still convinced that the minimalist approach is the best. After all, in the kitchen your best equipment is your hands. I use my (clean) hands as much as I can: to pat seasoning into meat and fish, to tear large leaves, to toss salads (preferably in large shallow bowls), to add pinches of this and that . . . I am gradually weaning myself away from dipping a finger in food to taste it, but it's hard work.

To cook *Fast French* you need a standard *batterie de cuisine* with which you feel thoroughly comfortable. The last thing you want is to be assembling an array of unfamiliar appliances and utensils before you embark on cooking a dish. I will assume you have a reliable cooker with good heat control, a grill, and perhaps a cast iron griddle – perfect for fast searing of meat *à la française*.

If you haven't got one already, I strongly recommend that you invest in a food processor, preferably one that has two different-sized bowls. The more I use mine the more I realize how invaluable and liberating it is when you are trying to cook fast.

You need a good set of knives, a couple of pairs of scissors for snipping food into easy-to-cook pieces, several chopping boards (including one dedicated to raw meat), large and small whisks, a zester to strip off thin shreds of citrus peel, a strong pastry- or paint-brush for coating ingredients, a heatproof spatula and a few wooden spoons. I also have a wooden fork which looks like a child's toy rather than a grown-up utensil. It is great for stirring and turning food in the sauté pan.

Another much-used gadget is a salad spinner which gets leaves dry in seconds. I also go through roll after roll of recycled absorbent paper, perfect for patting off excess moisture from ingredients and miscellaneous jobs such as wiping or greasing pans, skimming off grey surface foam from simmering liquids, etc . . .

Halfway between a frying pan and a saucepan, the sauté pan is probably the best all round cooking pot when you are in a hurry. It has a wide heavy base on which food can be spread in a single layer and cooked in minutes. It enables liquids to evaporate quickly and sauces to reduce in moments. With its lid on, it speeds up the making of soups and fricasses.

Still on the pan front, you really need 2 solid saucepans, a large one and a small one, and pair of non-stick frying pans – again one large and one small. The more non-stick the coating of your frying pan, the less fat you will need to use. I also have an omelette pan that I reserve for cooking eggs and pancakes.

Perhaps because I was brought up in a country where water tends to be boiled in a saucepan with a lid on top, I have become addicted to my jug kettle. This splendid appliance boils just the amount of water required and saves several minutes several times a day, not just when brewing up but also when ingredients need to be simmered or poached. Just pour enough boiling water to cover the ingredients into the pan.

Last but not least, when time is short it helps not to have to transfer the food to a serving dish. Whenever feasible, I present the food in the pot or pan in which it was cooked.

TECHNIQUES

Preparation

Whenever you want to speed up your cooking, remember that small is beautiful. Smaller pieces of food will obviously cook faster than large ones. Cut ingredients down to the size you want (as it happens, very often bite-size works well in fast cooking) with a sharp knife on the chopping board, or use scissors to snip food straight into the pan (particularly ham, bacon and herbs). Have fun experimenting with batch cutting, ie lining up several items on the board and slicing them with one fell swoop of a large cook's knife. Also worth trying, particularly if you were brought up to top and tail *haricots verts* one by one, is snipping a handful of beans at a time. Knock them against the chopping board first at one end and then the other to level them and minimize waste.

When you use the food processor, cut or snip ingredients to even-sized pieces, no bigger than about 2.5cm/1in. First whizz the ingredients with the harder texture for a few seconds until coarsely chopped, then add the softer pieces, whizz again, then trickle in the liquid and whizz again – briefly. A few seconds is a long time in food processing: it is as easy to over-blend as it is for golden toast to turn inedible charcoal black.

COOKING

Pan-frying First heat the pan until very hot to 'quick start' the cooking process and seize the meat or fish. Reduce the heat a little (more in the case of fish), but keep it moderately high to prevent the meat stewing in its own juices. Turn over the food halfway through cooking, pat down to seize the raw side and cook as before.

Deglaze the pan to make a mini-sauce: first remove the meat or fish, turn up the heat, add in a little acidic liquid (usually wine – be mean: a few tablespoons go a long way at this stage) and stir to mix with the pan juices. When you are ready to take the pan off the heat, whisk in a few small knobs of chilled butter or a spoonful of cream, Greek-style yogurt or fromage frais. Adjust the seasoning.

Sautéeing Start with a hot pan, reduce the heat a little and keep stirring the food as suggested in the recipe. Stirring frequency ranges from once or twice to fairly frequently, but on the whole it is not as steady as in stir-frying.

Grilling Always preheat the grill to high, then reduce the heat to suit the recipe and keep an eye on what happens at all times.

Poaching Bring the cooking liquid to the boil before you add the ingredients. As soon as tiny bubbles reappear, reduce the heat and never let the liquid do more than quiver a little.

Simmering Allow the odd discreet small bubbles, but too much heat will toughen delicate ingredients.

Boiling is much more vigorous. Whatever the degree of heat, never use more water than you need. An extra 2.5cm/1in of liquid on top of the ingredients is the maximum for fast cooking. If it evaporates too quickly, add a little extra boiling water and reduce the heat. As always, it is easier to add than subtract. Soups are diluted with extra liquid at the end of cooking.

Reducing cooking liquid is the most usual way of making a sauce. First, lift out the main ingredients and keep them warm. Turn up the heat under the pan and boil vigorously for a minute, or 2 or 3 – this is when a wide sauté pan really comes its own. After this rather drastic intervention, loosen and soften the thickened sauce with a few spoonfuls of not too acidic liquid (say, orange juice or fortified wine). All your sauce now needs is a touch of butter to make it shine. Check the seasoning before serving.

INGREDIENTS

Vive le marché! The traditional French food shopping pattern has always been little and often. In these days of supermarkets, this means topping up the basic big weekly shopping trip with regular visits to trusted specialist retailers.

Most of the ingredients you need to cook *Fast French* should be available in larger quality supermarkets with a fresh fish counter, a decent deli department and a selection of well boned and trimmed meat. Avoid the ready-to-eat cabinets and instead go for convenience with skinned and filleted fish, washed and cut vegetables and salads. I cannot guarantee that you will find every single ingredient mentioned in this book in your supermarket, particularly when it comes to a few of the condiments, but I have used nothing that I could not find without too much trouble in a well-stocked specialist deli or good Oriental store. Condiments tend to last a few months anyway, so they justify the odd little expedition . . .

Herbs and vegetables To my mind, parsley and tarragon are the most French of herbs, then come chives and chervil. I always have a bunch of flat leaf parsley at hand in the kitchen, either growing in a little pot on the window sill, or trimmed in a sealed jar in the refrigerator. Herbs are best fresh, but some dried herbs work fine – unfortunately with the exception of parsley, chives and chervil. Replace your stock of dried herbs every few months since they lose their fullness of flavour very quickly. Use them more sparingly than you would fresh herbs, otherwise your dish will end up tasting somewhat synthetic.

Garlic is inevitably associated with French cooking. I won't dwell on it here except to say that it should be used fresh and sparingly unless it happens to be the spirit of the dish. Much more neglected in home kitchens outside France is the shallot, delicately sharp and a wonderful enhancer of flavour – whether with potatoes, butter sauces, beef or tomatoes to mention but a few examples of its many uses. It keeps well, wrapped in the salad compartment of the refrigerator. Spring onions are also a reliable and versatile staple in fast cooking. The white part quickly imparts that special 'onion' taste to a dish at the start of the cooking, while the green part snips decoratively in the later stages.

Fresh young – but not premature – vegetables are best for *Fast French,* ideally when they are in season. I am not a great freezer user, but I usually have small packets of frozen spinach, broad beans and baby garden peas in stock.

Condiments I like to use sea salt, both coarse and fine, since a little of it goes a long way. Black peppercorns get milled very steadily in my kitchen. More interesting still in fast cooking is the clean sharp taste of lightly crushed green peppercorns. Buy them in bottled brine and keep the jar in the refrigerator. Another condiment that is always present *chez moi* in the said refrigerator is harissa, a very hot (but not bitter) chilli and spice paste from North Africa. I use it frequently. You may need to make a special trip to a specialist store to find it. It is easiest to use squeezed out of a tube (looking dangerously like tomato paste as I once learnt to my disadvantage) but often comes in a small can. Transfer to a small clean screw-top jar after opening and keep chilled. Use minuscule amounts. Capers are another favourite condiment, as is paprika, lemon pepper, soy sauce, Worcestershire sauce and Tabasco. I also use anchovy paste, tomato paste, and, discreetly, tomato ketchup and mushroom ketchup. Mustards (French and English, coarse and smooth) are worth their shelf space, as are vinegars (red and white wine, sherry and balsamic and perhaps raspberry) but I draw the line at chi-chi flavours. Vinegars should perhaps be measured in drops rather than spoonfuls – use them with a very light touch.

Fats Unsalted creamery butter is the most appropriate for *Fast French,* but slightly salted butter is fine unless otherwise stated. Crème fraîche with its ripe but slightly tart taste is, of course, the *crème de la crème* of French cooking. It is not always available, nor is soured cream which is a good (but tarter still) alternative. Rather than using double cream in recipes that call for crème fraîche, I prefer to replace it with a mixture of fromage frais (not the very low-fat variety, which I find frankly disappointing to cook with) and Greek-style yogurt. Stirring a couple of tablespoons of the cooking liquid into the fromage frais and yogurt mixture before you whisk it into the pan helps the texture of the sauce. Groundnut and sunflower oils vie for shelf space in the French store cupboard. I use either. It is worthwhile storing two kinds of olive oil; a standard supermarket bottle for general purposes, and a bottle of extra virgin oil for special occasions where flavour really matters. Walnut oil is splendid fresh, but does not keep and I only buy it in small bottles. All oils are best kept in a cool dark place.

Wine and drinks *Fast French* uses a little wine and, on occasions, a dash of cognac or brandy in sauces. The wine that goes into the sauce is traditionally the one you serve with the dish. Madeira is a popular fortified wine in France and a brilliant cooking aid. Unlike dry wine, it can be added towards the end of cooking and gives sauces and dishes a deep sweet dark flavour. Cointreau is good in desserts, as are kirsch and *crème de cassis*. Another magnificent adjunct to desserts, if not a dessert in its own right, is some *Pruneaux d'Agen à l'Armagnac*, very superior prunes soaked in very superior brandy.

Bread French bread is not known for its keeping qualities. In addition to fresh bread, I also often have a brioche loaf in the refrigerator. Brioche will keep for a good 10 days and is much easier to slice and use once it is chilled and slightly stale. I also store a container of Pillsbury's chilled croissant dough for weekend breakfasts and impromptu snacks or starters (see page 48).

Rice, pasta and other grains In addition to rice and small macaroni-style dried pasta, I keep a packet of bulgur (cracked wheat) in the store cupboard. It fluffs up in minutes when moistened, absorbs seasonings like a sponge and tastes a little nutty. Couscous is another possibility – you can find both in health food stores, if not in supermarkets.

Cans Chopped plum tomatoes, white haricot beans, flageolets, tuna in oil, anchovy fillets in oil and petits pois are all worth storing.

Other miscellaneous ingredients in the store cupboard Marmalade and mixed berry preserves are useful cooking ingredients. I also store bitter chocolate with a high cocoa content. Dried nuts have a limited shelf life but, provided you remember it is there, a small packet of slivered almonds, pine nuts or walnuts can be put to good use before it turns rancid. In the refrigerator, I always have lardons (see page 61) or smoked streaky bacon, thin slices of dry-cured ham and a chunk of *saucisson* as well as a jar of small pickled gherkins, a couple of unwaxed lemons and limes, a bottle or pack of freshly squeezed orange juice, a piece of strong Gruyère or Parmesan and several fresh eggs. In the freezer, I tuck in a packet of ready-to-roll puff pastry sheets and small portions of stock.

On the subject of stock Stock-making takes too long for *Fast French*, but there are various ways to deal with the problem. To start with the easy gourmet option, many supermarkets sell tubs of delicious chilled stocks with a rich well-balanced flavour. I buy them when I see them – they tend to be expensive. Once I get home, I chill half and freeze the rest.

Less satisfying but still fine-flavoured and a great deal cheaper are the new gourmet stock cubes you can buy in both health food stores and leading supermarkets. They are far less salty than the traditional old cubes. Some stores also sell court bouillon sachets, a spice and herb mixture that is used for poaching fish and seafood.

A perfectly adequate 'stock effect' can be achieved in moments by adding a little soy sauce to the cooking liquid. Start with a scant tablespoonful, taste and add more soy sauce if necessary. The pan juices left after sautéeing mushrooms also make a nice (mushroom-flavoured) stock base.

If you have the time and inclination, a basic chicken stock is easily made by simmering 2 very ordinary birds in a large saucepan with plenty of water, a few peppercorns, a pinch of sea salt, a chopped onion, a leek, a chopped carrot and maybe a stalk of celery or a few strips of lemon zest. After 50 minutes or so remove the white breast meat (delicious with Basil mayonnaise, (see page 16) and continue simmering for an hour and a half. Leave to cool in the pan, remove the carcasses and pass the stock through a muslin-lined sieve. Adjust the seasoning.

To make a light fish stock, simmer together in a sauté pan with 5cm/2in water a few chopped mushrooms, a finely sliced leek, a chopped shallot, a few fennel seeds or a pinch of thyme (optional), a little grated lemon zest and a few peppercorns. After 15 minutes, throw in some crustacean shells and some white fish trimmings (from non-oily fish). Bring back to a simmer and cook for 15 minutes. Strain through a fine sieve and adjust the seasoning.

Use the same method without the crustacean shells and fish trimmings to make vegetable stock, adding a chopped onion, a stalk of celery and a tomato.

À chacun son goût . . . some people prefer their food more spiced, seasoned or strongly flavoured and some are more concerned than others about fat and cholesterol content. Whenever particularly appropriate, measurements and ingredients are flexible (e.g. '4-6 tbsp', '1-2 garlic cloves', 'crème fraîche or fromage frais'). Err on the side of caution if you are trying a recipe for the first time or if you are watching your diet. When there is a choice (e.g. 'several sprigs of chives or dill'), the first alternative tends to reflect my preference, but let availability be your guide. All the recipes are to be enjoyed rather than rigidly adhered to.

RECETTES PASSE-PARTOUT

The following recipes are favourite standbys and part of my constant repertoire. I rely on them to liven up all manner of plain food with very little effort in my part.

PETIT SAUCE CITRONNÉE

Quick Lemon Sauce

This delicate sauce is good with poached fish. I also like it with chicken breasts, poached in a light stock with the white parts of a few spring onions and a handful of chopped mushrooms. For a zingy alternative, try fresh tarragon instead of parsley.

SERVES 3-4 • UNDER 20 MINUTES

2 tsp groundnut oil
30-45 g/1-1½ oz butter
1 shallot, finely chopped
few sprigs of flat leaf parsley
2 scant tsp cornflour
100 ml/3½ fl oz Fish or Chicken stock (see page 13) or
    poaching liquid
5 tbsp dry white wine
1 tbsp finely grated zest and about 1 tbsp juice from
    an unwaxed lemon
3 tbsp crème fraîche, fromage frais or single cream
1 small egg yolk
sea salt and freshly ground black pepper

1   While your fish or chicken is cooking, heat the oil in a small saucepan and stir in two-thirds of the butter. When the butter starts sizzling, add the shallots and snip in a little parsley. Season lightly and stir for a minute or two over a moderate heat.

2 Sprinkle in the cornflour, stir for a few seconds, then dribble in the stock or cooking liquid and the wine, beating vigorously. Sprinkle in the lemon zest and bring to a simmer, still stirring.

3 Simmer for a few minutes, stirring occasionally, then stir in the crème fraîche, fromage frais or cream and reduce the heat a little.

4 In a cup, combine the egg yolk with the lemon juice and a couple of spoonfuls of the hot sauce. Whisk this egg mixture back into the pan of sauce and continue whisking for a minute.

5 Just before serving, whisk the rest of the butter into the sauce. Adjust the seasoning, adding a little extra lemon juice if liked. Snip in a little more parsley and serve the sauce piping hot in a small warmed bowl or sauce boat.

SAUCE À L'OSEILLE

Sorrel Sauce

This sharp short sauce suits most grilled and poached fish, especially oily ones like salmon and trout.

SERVES 2 • UNDER 20 MINUTES

about 85 g/3 oz fresh young sorrel leaves
several sprigs of flat leaf parsley
few soft lettuce leaves
45 g/1½ oz chilled butter, diced
3 tbsp light stock or poaching liquid
3 tbsp crème fraîche or Greek-style yogurt
sea salt and freshly ground black pepper

1 While the fish is cooking, make the sauce: first prepare the leaves, remove the ribs from the larger sorrel leaves, snip off the leaves from the parsley stalks and roll up and snip the lettuce leaves across into strips.

2 Heat half the butter over a very low heat in a small heavy pan. Tip in the leaves and stir until darkened and melting. Stir in the stock or cooking liquid, followed by the crème fraîche or yogurt. Season the sauce lightly and keep it hot until the fish is on the plates ready to be served.

3 To serve: whisk the rest of the butter into the sauce and spoon it over the fish.

MAYONNAISE

Golden rich mayonnaise is good served with assorted poached fish, cold meats, hard-boiled eggs or quails' eggs, crudités and tiny boiled new potatoes. It is much more likely to emulsify smoothly and in the given time if all your ingredients are at room temperature.

SERVES 4 • UNDER 15 MINUTES

1 large egg yolk
1 tbsp French mustard
1 tsp red or white wine vinegar
about 200 ml/7 fl oz groundnut oil or 150 ml/¼ pt
    groundnut oil and 3 tbsp strong olive oil
few drops of lemon juice
sea salt and freshly ground black pepper

1 Put the egg yolk in a large bowl. Season lightly with salt and pepper and add the mustard and vinegar without stirring. (If your ingredients are not at room temperature, cover with a very thin film of oil and leave to stand for at least 15 minutes without stirring.)

2 Wedge the bowl in place on a mat of dampened paper towels. Whisk the egg and other ingredients until well combined – I use an electric whisk, but it can be done with a balloon whisk or even a wooden spoon and plenty of elbow-grease.

3 Still whisking, trickle in a few drops of oil. As soon as the oil has blended into the mixture, trickle in a little more, still whisking.

4 Continue adding the oil very slowly a few drops at a time until the mixture thickens, then start pouring in a continuous thin trickle, still whisking until the mayonnaise emulsifies. If you are using olive oil, start whisking it in once you have used up the groundnut oil.

5 Carry on whisking until you have a glossy thick mayonnaise. Taste and adjust the seasoning, adding a few drops of lemon juice. Cover and chill until needed.

To make **Garlic Mayonnaise,** crush a large juicy garlic clove (or more if you prefer) and add it to the egg yolk and other ingredients before you start whisking.
For a quick **Rouille** (the spicy Provençal mayonnaise, popular with fish soups), add a little crushed garlic and a dollop of harissa (no bigger than a hazelnut) to the ingredients before you start whisking. Whisk in 2 or 3 teaspoons of tomato paste once your mayonnaise has emulsified. Season with paprika or cayenne pepper.

HOLLANDAISE MINUTE

Quick Hollandaise

This fast rendering of the classic sauce is a real doddle – but you do need a food processor. It is perfect with poached fish and asparagus.

SERVES 4 • UNDER 10 MINUTES

1 tbsp white wine vinegar
2 small or 1 large egg yolks
about 150 g/5½ oz soft unsalted butter
sea salt and fresh ground black pepper

1 In a small saucepan, boil the vinegar with 4 tablespoons of water until reduced to about 1 tablespoon.

2 Whizz the egg yolks or yolk in the food processor until smooth. Tip in the reduced vinegar and whizz again for a few seconds.

3 Put the butter in the saucepan and melt over a very low heat.

4 With the food processor running, trickle the melted butter into the yolk mixture. Whizz until the sauce thickens and season to your liking with salt and pepper.

CROÛTONS À L'AIL

Garlic Croutons

If you prefer not to use garlic, omit and use the same method to prepare plain croutons. Grated Parmesan, mashed anchovy fillets, a smattering of tomato paste or a sprinkling of pungent dried herbs can be added to the oil-coated bread to make flavoured croûtes (if the topping is substantial, serve whole rather than as bite-sized croutons). These are good as appetizers, or with soups and salads.

SERVES 4 • UNDER 10 MINUTES

4 slices of good quality day-old bread, crusts
**   removed if too thick**
1 juicy garlic clove, halved
1½ tbsp extra virgin olive oil, plus extra if needed sea
salt and freshly ground black pepper

1 Preheat the grill to high. Reduce the heat and grill the slices of bread for a minute or two on each side until crisp but barely coloured. Remove the bread but leave the grill on.

2 Flatten the garlic clove halves, cut side down, with the flat of a large knife. Rub the cut sides of the crushed cloves all over the bread.

3 Put the olive oil in a small plate, swirling the plate to spread the oil. Put a slice of bread on the plate, turn over to coat both sides with oil. Repeat this procedure with the other slices of bread, adding extra olive oil if necessary.

4 Season lightly and grill until golden. Cut into small squares no larger than 4 cm/½ in before serving or leave whole if using as croûtes as described above.

PETITE CRÈME

Flavoured Cream

This all-purpose flavoured cream is good with soft summer fruit, berries and fruit tarts (see page 125). Other flavourings for the cream work well too: try finely grated lime or lemon zest, chopped mint leaves or chopped stem ginger in syrup.

SERVES 4 • UNDER 5 MINUTES, PLUS CHILLING

4 heaped tbsp chilled fromage frais or whipping
**   cream**
4 heaped tbsp chilled Greek-style yogurt
1-2 tbsp milk
2 tsp finely grated zest from an unwaxed orange
2-3 tbsp Cointreau, kirsch or other fruit liqueur
**   (optional, but recommended)**
icing sugar to taste

1 Whisk together the fromage frais or cream and the yogurt. Thin down with a little milk. Stir in the orange zest and the liqueur, if using.

2 Sweeten to taste with a little icing sugar and chill until needed.

3 Just before serving, adjust the flavouring and consistency with a little more sugar, milk or alcohol if necessary.

SOUPES
et
HORS D'ŒUVRE

*A small fresh plate of crudités at
lunch time, a bowl of
warming soup in the evening . . . no
self-respecting French meal
is complete without a light
first course.*

POTAGE AU CRESSON

Watercress Soup

SERVES 2-3 • UNDER 30 MINUTES

1 slice of rindless smoked bacon or 2 tsp oil
1 waxy potato, weighing about 170 g/6 oz, chopped
  into small pieces
250 ml/8 fl oz Chicken or Vegetable Stock (see the
  Introduction on page 13)
100 g/3½ oz sachet of trimmed and washed
  watercress
15-30 g/½-1 oz butter
2 generous tsp Greek-style yogurt
sea salt and freshly ground black pepper

1 Bring a kettle of water to the boil. Heat a medium
heavy saucepan over a moderate heat. Snip in the
bacon, if using, and sauté until golden, stirring
occasionally. If not using bacon, swirl the oil into the
hot pan.

2 Add the potato pieces to the pan and stir to coat
them with fat. Pour in the stock and add just enough
boiling water to cover. Season with salt and pepper and
turn up the heat.

3 When the liquid starts bubbling, turn down the heat
and add the watercress. Cover tightly and simmer for
10-15 minutes, until the potato is cooked.

4 Whizz the mixture in the food processor until
smooth. Return to the pan over a low heat. Adjust the
seasoning and texture, adding a little more boiling water
if necessary.

5 Pour into warmed soup bowls, stir a knob of butter
and a teaspoon of yogurt into each and serve
immediately.

GRATINÉE EXPRESS

Quick Onion Soup

SERVES 2 • UNDER 30 MINUTES

½ tbsp oil
30 g/1 oz butter
1 large sweet white onion or the white parts of 5
  large spring onions, finely sliced
400 ml/14 fl oz Chicken or Vegetable Stock, or
  alternative (see page 13)
100 ml/3½ fl oz not-too-dry white wine
75 g/2½ oz good Gruyère or Emmental cheese, grated
6 small slices of baguette-style bread
sea salt and freshly ground black pepper

1 In a sauté pan, heat the oil over a moderate heat.
Add the butter, swirl it around as it melts, then tip in the
onion. Turn up the heat. Season lightly and sauté for a
few minutes, stirring frequently, until the onion is
golden brown.

2 Pour in the stock and wine and bring to the boil.
Reduce the heat and cover. Simmer gently for at least
12 minutes – a little longer if time allows.

3 Meanwhile, preheat the grill to high and spread the
grated cheese over the slices of bread. Season with
pepper.

4 Divide the cooked onion between 2 flameproof
bowls. Pour the broth into them and top with the
prepared bread, cheese side up.

5 Grill until the cheese bubbles and serve at once.

TOP *Potage au Cresson*
BOTTOM *Gratinée Express*

SOUPE FRAÎCHE À L'AVOCAT ET À LA TOMATE

Chilled Avocado and Tomato Soup

A summer favourite, this soup was first concocted en famille to put to good use a glut of tomatoes and herbs – together with the brand new food processor for which my father was reluctant to find room in his kitchen. The avocado takes the acidic edge off the flavour, but the combination of ingredients is very flexible. Pushing the tomatoes through a sieve may seem fastidious in fast cooking, but it really does transform the texture.

SERVES 6 • UNDER 15 MINUTES

550 g/1¼ lb ripe tomatoes, quartered
1 garlic clove, chopped
2 smallish ripe avocados, peeled, stoned and
   chopped
juice of ½ lemon
several sprigs of fresh herbs, such as parsley, chervil,
   chives, thyme and basil
pinch each of dried ground coriander and cumin
chilled water
¼ tsp harissa or a few drops of Tabasco sauce
175 ml/6 fl oz fromage frais (or a mixture of
   Greek-style yogurt and fromage frais)
sea salt and freshly ground black pepper
ice cubes, to serve

1 Whizz the tomatoes in the food processor and then press the resulting purée through a sieve·into a bowl or a large jug.

2 Put the garlic, avocados, herbs and spices in the food processor, reserving some sprigs of herbs for garnish. Season lightly and whizz briefly to mix.

3 Pour in the tomato purée and add the fromage frais or yogurt mixture. Whizz again to blend and then thin down with chilled water until the texture is to your liking. Adjust the seasoning and flavour with more harissa or Tabasco to taste.

4 Just before serving, add a few ice cubes to each bowl and snip in a few sprigs of fresh herbs.

VELOUTÉ À L'ÉPINARD

Creamy Spinach Soup

A very simple velouté . . . I love the combination of the flavours of spinach and zingy goats' cheese, but the soup is perhaps more mellow and 'safer' for first-time users when made with cream cheese.

SERVES 4 • UNDER 30 MINUTES

2 tsp oil
1 waxy potato, weighing about 170 g/6 oz, cut into
   small pieces
350 g/12 oz sachet of trimmed and washed baby
   spinach
pinch of freshly grated nutmeg
few drops of Tabasco sauce
dash of soy sauce
4 generous tbsp cream cheese or very fresh soft
   goats' cheese, plus extra to finish
sea salt and freshly ground black pepper

1 Bring a kettle of water to the boil.

2 Put the oil in a heavy saucepan or sauté pan over a moderate heat. Add the potato, season and stir for a minute to coat with the oil.

3 Pour into the pan enough of the boiling water to cover, bring to a simmer and cook for 5-8 minutes.

4 Add the spinach, reserving a few leaves. Season with a little nutmeg, a few drops of Tabasco and a dash of soy sauce. Cook for about 5 minutes, until the vegetables are just tender.

5 Return the kettle to the boil. Meanwhile, spoon the cream cheese into the soup and stir.

6 Whizz the soup in the food processor.

7 Return the soup to the pan. Whizz a little hot water in the food processor to rinse it out and tip into the soup.

8 Adjust the seasoning and the consistency, adding more boiling water if necessary.

9 Pour the soup into warmed bowls. Swirl in a small dollop of cream cheese, snip in a few of the reserved spinach leaves and season with a little extra pepper.

PETITE SOUPE AU PISTOU

Quick Vegetable and Pasta Soup with
Basil Mayonnaise

*This robust soup is a meal in itself, with the added
benefit of being unobtrusively vegetarian.*

*The Basil Mayonnaise is a great all-purpose pasta and
vegetable sauce. Add chopped shallot and capers and
serve with Pot au Feu Minute (see page 82) or use to
liven up the boiled chicken produced while making
stock (see page 13).*

SERVES 4-6 • UNDER 30 MINUTES

2 tbsp olive oil
2 large spring onions, chopped
2 garlic cloves, crushed
400 g/14 oz canned chopped tomatoes and their
    juice
about 350 g/12 oz mixed baby vegetables
    (courgettes, carrots, mange-tout peas), chopped
55 g/2 oz frozen baby broad beans
170 g/6 oz small hard pasta, such as mini macaroni
170 g/6 oz canned haricot beans or red kidney beans,
    drained
55 g/2 oz strong Gruyère or Parmesan cheese, grated
sea salt and freshly ground black pepper
Garlic Croutons (see page 17), to serve

FOR THE BASIL MAYONNAISE
1 egg
1 tsp Dijon mustard
100 ml/3½ fl oz groundnut or sunflower oil
5 tbsp olive oil
2 tsp wine vinegar
1 generous tbsp cream
several sprigs of parsley
several leaves of basil

1 Bring a kettle of water to the boil. Heat the oil in a
large heavy saucepan or sauté pan. Add the onions and
garlic and stir over a moderate heat for a few minutes.

2 Tip in the tomatoes and their juice. Stir and season
lightly.

3 Add the chopped vegetables. Cover with boiling
water, stir and bring to a simmer.

4 Sprinkle in the pasta and add enough boiling water to
cover with 2.5 cm/1 in above the pasta. Bring back to a
simmer.

5 Cook for about 12 minutes, until the pasta is almost
tender. Tip in the beans and heat through.

6 While the soup is cooking, make the Basil
Mayonnaise: boil the egg for 3 minutes, then scoop out
the yolk into a large bowl and reserve the white.

7 Beat the yolk with a pinch of salt, the mustard and
vinegar. Using an electric whisk, beat in the vegetable
oil a few drops at a time, then in a thin trickle. Add the
olive oil in the same way. Once all the oil has been
incorporated, beat in the cream to make a thinnish
mayonnaise.

8 Chop up the egg white and stir this into the sauce.
Snip in plenty of parsley and basil and season lightly
with salt and more generously with pepper.

9 Just before serving the soup, adjust the seasoning if
necessary and lightly stir the cheese into the soup. Serve
with Garlic Croutons and dollops of the Basil
Mayonnaise.

SALADE DE TOMATES AUX PETITS OIGNONS

Tomato and Onion Salad

SERVES 4 • UNDER 20 MINUTES

2 large or 4 medium ripe tomatoes
the white parts of 2 large spring onions (or 1 shallot)
several sprigs of chervil and/or flat leaf parsley
3 tbsp olive oil
2 tsp white wine vinegar or lemon juice
coarse sea salt and freshly ground black pepper
fresh crusty bread, to serve

1 Thinly slice the tomatoes, removing the seeds and some of the core and pulp if wished.

2 Starting from the centre, arrange the tomato slices in overlapping circles on a round platter.

3 Cut the spring onion into very thin rings, or chop the shallot finely, and scatter over the tomatoes. Season with a sprinkling of coarse salt and pepper.

4 Snip over a little chervil and/or parsley.

5 Whisk together the oil and vinegar or lemon juice. Season this dressing lightly and dribble it over the tomatoes.

6 Leave the salad to stand at room temperature for a few minutes before serving accompanied by bread to mop up the juices.

CHOU RÂPÉ

Raw Cabbage Salad

SERVES 4 • UNDER 15 MINUTES

1 small white or red cabbage (or a mixture),
**   quartered and cored**
4-6 tbsp groundnut or sunflower oil
1 tbsp red wine vinegar
sea salt and freshly ground black pepper
½ tsp mild mustard
sprig of thyme

1 First make the dressing: in a cup, whisk together the oil, vinegar and mustard. Season generously and snip in the thyme.

2 Grate the cabbage using the shredding disc of the food processor. If you prefer, use a sharp knife to cut it into long thin shreds.

3 Toss the cabbage shreds with the dressing until well coated. If time allows, leave the salad to stand for a while before serving.

CAROTTES RÂPÉES

Shredded Carrots

Add a handful of stoned black olives and some thick wedges of hard-boiled egg for a more substantial – and even more colourful – salad.

SERVES 4 • UNDER 20 MINUTES

400 g/14 oz mature firm carrots, peeled
4-5 tbsp olive oil, plus extra if liked
1 tbsp juice and ½ tsp finely grated zest from an
**   unwaxed orange**
juice of 1 lemon
several sprigs of flat leaf parsley
sprig of tarragon
sea salt and freshly ground black pepper

1 Using the shredding disc of the food processor, grate the carrots. If you use a grater, grate on the slant to get longer shreds.

2 In a cup, combine the oil, orange juice and zest and lemon juice, reserving 1-2 teaspoons of lemon juice. Season to taste.

3 Toss the carrot shreds with the dressing until well coated. Leave to stand for a good few minutes if time allows.

4 Just before serving, snip in the herbs, season again lightly and sprinkle with the reserved lemon juice and an extra trickle of olive oil, if liked (the salad should be quite moist).

TERRINE DE SAUMON FUMÉ

Smoked Salmon Pâté

SERVES 4 • UNDER 25 MINUTES

150 g/5½ oz smoked salmon, snipped
2 sprigs of fresh thyme, finely snipped
juice and finely grated zest of ½ small unwaxed
   lemon
55 g/2 oz soft unsalted butter
1 tbsp groundnut oil
4 tbsp thick Greek-style yogurt
paprika
freshly ground black pepper

TO SERVE
4 slices of toasted brioche
butter
salad leaves lightly dressed with a sprinkling of
   groundnut oil and a little sea salt

1 Whizz the salmon in the food processor with the
thyme, lemon juice and zest for a few seconds.

2 Add the butter, oil and yogurt and season lightly with
pepper and paprika. Whizz briefly until combined.

3 Adjust the seasoning and stir in a little extra paprika.
Serve on individual plates, with a slice of buttered
toasted brioche and some lightly dressed salad leaves.

MOUSSE DE FOIES DE VOLAILLE TRICHEUSE

Cheat's Chicken Liver Pâté

*At the Auberge de la Brenne near Châteaurenault in
north Touraine, Ghislaine Salé serves a mousse de foies
de volailles that is rich, smooth and deep-flavoured. It
melts in the mouth in a totally satisfying way. Necessity
being the mother of invention, I tried to recreate my
friend's delectable concoction one evening when I felt
depressed by a rather sad slab of chicken liver pâté from
some local deli. The result is not quite the real thing, but
is good enough for guests to demand the recipe.*

SERVES 4 • UNDER 30 MINUTES

100 g/3½ oz bought chicken liver pâté
45 g/1½ oz soft unsalted butter
1 tbsp fromage frais, crème fraîche or cream cheese
1 tbsp Madeira or port
1½ tsp brandy
cayenne pepper
Tabasco sauce
Worcestershire sauce
mushroom ketchup or 6 green peppercorns
   (optional)
fingers of hot toast or toasted brioche, to serve

1 Cut the chicken liver pâté into small pieces.

2 In a food processor, whizz together the pâté, butter,
fromage frais or crème fraîche or cream cheese,
Madeira or port and the brandy for a few seconds.

3 Taste and season to your liking with a small sprinkling
of cayenne, a couple of drops each of Tabasco,
Worcestershire sauce and mushroom ketchup or the
green peppercorns, if using. Whizz again briefly to mix
and chill for 15 minutes, or until needed.

4 Serve with fingers of hot toast or toasted brioche.

PREVIOUS PAGES
LEFT *Chou Râpé*
TOP RIGHT *Salade de Tomates aux Petits Oignons*
BOTTOM RIGHT *Carottes Râpées*

FONDS D'ARTICHAUT SURPRISE

Stuffed Artichoke Bottoms

SERVES 4 • UNDER 20 MINUTES

4-8 (depending on size) canned artichoke bottoms, drained
1 tbsp olive oil
2 thin slices of dry-cured Parma, Bayonne or Serrano ham
few drops of Tabasco sauce
2 generous tbsp cream cheese or fromage frais
45 g/1½ oz strong Gruyère, mature Cheddar or fresh Parmesan cheese, grated
freshly ground black pepper

1 Preheat the grill to high. Season the concave sides of the artichoke bottoms with pepper and brush them lightly with oil.

2 Roll up the ham into tight cigar shapes and snip these across finely.

3 Put half the shredded ham in a bowl, sprinkle with a few drops of Tabasco, then combine with the cream cheese and half the grated cheese. Season with pepper.

4 Spread a dollop of the ham and cheese mixture over each artichoke. Top with the rest of the ham and grated cheese. Season again with pepper.

5 Grill for a few minutes until bubbling and serve hot.

ASPERGES ET TROIS PETITES SAUCES AU CHOIX

Easy Asparagus with a Choice of Three Sauces

Asparagus comes in many shapes and sizes. In 'my' part of the Loire the local variety tends to be fat and purple, with an all-too-brief season in the early spring. Friendly local restaurateurs whisper about asperges to their regulars and charge accordingly. I prepare it once a year – with great ceremony – and savour every glorious bite. The rest of the time I am very happy with the smaller and greener offerings of my local London market or supermarket.

The Egg and Shallot Vinaigrette is also good with leeks. Poach them, drain well, dress and serve tiède.

SERVES 4 • UNDER 25 MINUTES

450 g/1 lb thinnish asparagus
sea salt and freshly ground black pepper

FOR THE VINAIGRETTE À L'ÉCHALOTE
EGG AND SHALLOT VINAIGRETTE
2 eggs
1 small shallot, finely chopped
1 generous tsp Dijon mustard
100 ml/3½ fl oz groundnut or light olive oil
4 tsp red wine vinegar
several sprigs of flat leaf parsley

FOR THE MAYONNAISE À LA TOMATE ET À L'ESTRAGON
TOMATO TARRAGON MAYONNAISE
1 scant tsp Dijon mustard
1 tbsp good tomato paste
1 generous tbsp crème fraîche or fromage frais
175 ml/6 fl oz Mayonnaise (see page 16)
several sprigs of tarragon, finely snipped

FOR THE BEURRE FONDU AUX HERBES
HOT HERB BUTTER SAUCE
100 g/3½ oz unsalted butter, cut into pieces
several sprigs of chervil or chives
1½ tsp lemon juice
paprika

Fonds d'Artichaut Surprise

1 Start by making the cold sauces: to make the Egg and Shallot Vinaigrette, first hard-boil the eggs in a small saucepan with just enough water to cover for 8-10 minutes. Plunge them into very cold water for a few minutes, then shell them.

2 In a small bowl, mash the shallot with a good pinch of sea salt. Stir in the mustard, then whisk in the oil and the vinegar. Whisk until the mixture emulsifies. Season to taste.

3 Snip the parsley. Finely chop the egg whites and yolks, keeping them separate. If time allows, push them through a small sieve for a finer texture.

4 To make the Tomato Tarragon Mayonnaise: using a whisk or food processor, thoroughly whizz the mustard, tomato paste and crème fraîche into the Mayonnaise. Adjust the seasoning, but don't add the tarragon at this stage.

5 Cook the asparagus: bring about 5 cm/2 in salted water to the boil in a large sauté pan. Wash the asparagus. Cut off the tough ends, trimming the asparagus stalks to a length of 10-12 cm/4-5 in. Drop the stalks into the pan of boiling water, bring back to the boil and simmer for 4-6 minutes until just cooked.

6 While the asparagus is cooking, you can make the Hot Herb Butter Sauce: melt the butter over a low heat in a small heavy pan. Snip in the herbs, stir in the lemon juice and season to taste with salt, pepper and paprika.

7 Lift the asparagus out of the water with a fish slice, draining it well. Empty the pan and return it to a low heat. Spread the asparagus in the dry pan and carefully cook for a further 30-40 seconds – this will make the asparagus crisp and dry.

8 Lift the stalks out of the pan and fan them out on individual plates. Serve warm or at room temperature with crusty fresh bread and the sauce of your choice.

9 Either dribble the vinaigrette over the asparagus, then sprinkle alternating bands of egg white, parsley and egg yolk over it; or stir the tarragon into the mayonnaise just before serving; or dribble the hot butter sauce over the asparagus just before eating.

Asperges et Trois Petites Sauces au Choix

PLATS AUX ŒUFS

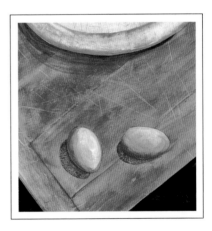

*Every day, in every café in the
land, hard-boiled eggs are
washed down with black coffee
as a basic but trusted way
of surviving until the
next proper meal.
What would French fast food
be sans oeufs?*

ŒUFS À LA COQUE GOURMANDE

Soft-boiled Eggs

*Take a newly laid egg fresh from the barn-yard, soft-boil
it to your liking and there you have it – gourmet heaven
in minutes. As a child on holiday at my grandparents in
the Touraine it was my favourite supper. Soldiers were
known as mouillettes and, if you were really hungry, you
were allowed two eggs. Œufs à la coque were a simple
treat and one we had frequently since there was a farm
next door and nobody had heard of cholesterol . . .
These days I make more of a fuss over exceptionally fresh
(less than 2 or 3 days old) free-range eggs. Served with
warm herbed mouillettes, and a spoonful of colourful
topping, they make the easiest of dinner party starters.*

SERVES 4 • UNDER 15 MINUTES

4 very fresh large free-range eggs
3 slices of top quality sandwich or brioche bread,
**   crusts removed**
55 g/2 oz soft butter
few sprigs each of parsley and chives or chervil
sea salt and freshly ground black pepper, to serve

FOR THE TOPPING

one of the following: 4 generous tsp salmon eggs;
30 g/1 oz smoked salmon, cut into slivers; 4 heaped
tsp crème fraîche; 4 heaped tsp soft butter mixed
with snipped tarragon, or with 4 snipped anchovy
fillets or 2 tsp green peppercorns

1 Preheat the grill and bring a kettle of water to the boil.

2 Put the eggs in a pan just big enough to hold them
and pour over the boiling water from the kettle. Soft-
boil the eggs in lightly bubbling water for 3-5 minutes,
depending on how well set you like them.

3 Meanwhile butter one side of each of the slices of
bread and grill until golden. While toasting, snip the herbs
into a saucer and prepare your topping, if necessary.

4 Butter and grill the other side of the bread. Cut each
grilled slice into 4 fingers. Coat each with the herbs.

5 Put each egg in an egg cup. Cut off the top of the egg
and spoon in a little of your chosen topping. Spoon a
little extra topping on the cut-off top. Serve each egg on
a pretty plate with an egg spoon and 3 *mouillettes*.
Have salt and pepper on the table.

PIPERADE

Shirred Eggs with Sweet Pepper and Tomato

*From France's Basque country, this dish is a very distant
relative of the Spanish tortilla which is good with pain de
campagne and a side salad. The end result should be
only lightly set.*

*One of my pet dislikes is undercooked sweet peppers:
if time allows or if I have them already prepared in the
fridge, I use Roasted Peppers (see Poivrons au Four on
page 103). If I have to start from scratch with a raw
piper (the Béarn word for pepper which gave its name to
the dish), I cut it into tiny strips and drain on a pile of
paper towels.*

SERVES 2 • UNDER 25 MINUTES

about 1½ tbsp olive oil, goose fat or bacon fat
3 large spring onions, green parts snipped and white
**   bulbs chopped**
1 small ripe red or yellow sweet pepper, deseeded
**   and cut into very small thin strips**
2-3 ripe tomatoes, blanched, skinned, deseeded and
**   chopped, or 175 g/6 oz canned chopped tomatoes,**
**   well drained**
1 garlic clove, chopped
pinch each of dried thyme and oregano
1 slice of dry-cured ham, finely snipped or cut
pinch of sugar (optional)
4 large eggs
sea salt and freshly ground black pepper

1 Swirl the oil or melt the fat in a heavy frying pan over
a moderate heat until the pan is well coated.

2 Tip in the spring onions and stir for a minute. Add the
pepper and tomatoes, stir and reduce the heat a little.

3 Stir in the garlic and herbs and cook for 5-8 minutes,
stirring occasionally, until the mixture softens.

4 Stir in the ham. Season to taste, adding a small pinch
of sugar if the mixture is too sharp.

5 Leave to simmer for a minute, while you break the
eggs into a bowl and beat them briskly with a fork.

6 Tip the eggs into the pan and stir over a low heat for
a few minutes, until the mixture is lightly set but still
moist. Serve immediately.

ŒUFS BROUILLÉS AUX FINES HERBES

Scrambled Eggs with Herbs

Never rush scrambled eggs. They will set perfectly well in their own sweet time – around 10-12 minutes – which can seem like forever to the cook in a hurry . . .

SERVES 2-3 • UNDER 20 MINUTES

4 large or 5 standard eggs
45 g/1½ oz unsalted butter
1 tbsp cream, fromage frais or milk
few sprigs of chervil or chives
sea salt and freshly ground black pepper
lightly toasted and buttered fingers or triangles of
    soft bread, crusts removed, to serve

1 Whisk the eggs lightly – they should not become fluffy.

2 In a heavy pan, melt half the butter over a low heat, swirling it around until the pan is well coated.

3 Cut the rest of the butter into small pieces.

4 Tip the eggs into the pan and cook gently, stirring very frequently with a wooden fork or spoon. Take the pan off the heat for a few seconds occasionally to keep the cooking slow.

5 While the eggs are setting, gradually stir in the rest of the butter, reserving one piece to finish.

6 When the eggs look just set and cooked, stir in the cream, fromage frais or milk.

7 Season to taste. Take the pan off the heat. Snip in the herbs and the last piece of butter. Stir and eat at once, with very lightly toasted soft bread.

ŒUFS BROUILLÉS AUX GIROLLES

Scrambled Eggs with Wild Mushrooms

SERVES 2-3 • UNDER 20 MINUTES

2 tsp groundnut oil
½ garlic clove
45 g/1½ oz unsalted butter
about 115 g/4 oz fresh chanterelles or other small
    wild mushrooms
4 large or 5 standard eggs
1 tbsp cream, fromage frais or milk
1 or 2 sprig(s) of parsley or a few chives
sea salt and freshly ground black pepper
very lightly toasted and buttered fingers or triangles
    of soft bread, crusts removed, to serve

1 Oil a heavy pan, then rub it with the cut side of the garlic.

2 Divide the butter into 3 pieces. Put a piece in the pan and melt it over a moderate heat, tipping the pan until well coated.

3 Add the mushrooms, season lightly and sauté for 2-3 minutes, stirring frequently.

4 Whisk the eggs lightly – they should not become fluffy.

5 Tip the sautéed mushrooms into a plate lined with paper towels.

6 Reduce the heat. Add half the remaining butter to the pan and swirl it around until melted.

7 Tip the eggs into the pan and cook gently, stirring very frequently with a wooden spoon or fork and taking the pan off the heat a few times to keep the cooking slow.

8 When the eggs look lightly set, sprinkle in the mushrooms and stir in the last piece of butter.

9 Take the pan off the heat, stir in the cream, fromage frais or milk and season lightly. Snip in the herbs and serve immediately, with very lightly toasted soft bread.

OVERLEAF
LEFT *Œufs Brouillés aux Girolles*
RIGHT *Œufs Brouillés aux Fines Herbes*

SOUFFLÉ AU ROQUEFORT

Blue Cheese Soufflé

The recipe below should produce a tasty soufflé that is crisp on the outside but still slightly gooey inside.

SERVES 2 AS A MAIN DISH, 4 AS A STARTER
• UNDER 45 MINUTES

30 g/1 oz butter, plus extra for greasing
30 g/1 oz flour
225 ml/7 fl oz milk
cayenne pepper
small pinch of freshly grated nutmeg
3 very fresh medium-to-large eggs, plus the white of
**   1 more egg, at room temperature**
85-100 g/3-3½ oz soft Roquefort or other strong blue
**   cheese, crumbled**
sea salt and freshly ground black pepper

1 Preheat the oven to 190C/375F/gas5. Generously butter the inside and rim of a 850 ml/1½ pt soufflé dish (about 15 cm/6 in across). Alternatively use two individual dishes about 10 cm/4 in across. Have all your other equipment and ingredients at hand.

2 In a heavy saucepan, melt the butter over a moderate heat. Tip in the flour and stir briskly until it is absorbed.

3 Gradually pour in the milk, a little at a time, beating well between additions. Beat frequently until the mixture bubbles. Season with a touch of cayenne, nutmeg, salt and pepper.

4 Reduce the heat a little and simmer for 3-4 minutes, beating occasionally. Turn off the heat and leave to cool for a few minutes, stirring occasionally.

5 Separate the eggs, keeping the whites free of any specks of yolk. Put the yolks in a small cup and the whites into a large mixing bowl. Whisk the whites until droopy peaks form.

6 Stir the cheese into the thick sauce. Trickle in the yolks and stir in well. Season with a little extra pepper.

7 Using a spatula or large metal spoon, fold about one-quarter of the whisked egg whites into the sauce. Tip this slackened sauce into the rest of the egg whites and fold them in lightly but thoroughly.

8 Pour the mixture into the prepared dish or dishes. Bake for about 25 minutes if in a single dish, 20 if in two dishes (without opening the oven door during the first 15-18 minutes in each case). The finished soufflés should be well risen and browned on the outside, but still very moist inside.

9 Serve immediately with a sharp green salad and chunks of fresh crusty bread.

ŒUFS AU PLAT SUR TARTINE

Fried Eggs on Savoury Toast

SERVES 2 • UNDER 20 MINUTES

2 thick slices of good sandwich bread
1 tsp groundnut oil
about 55 g/2 oz soft unsalted butter
2 small eggs
sea salt and freshly ground black pepper
tomato wedges, to garnish (optional)

1 Lightly butter and season the bread on both sides.

2 With a circular pastry cutter about 6 cm/2½ in diameter, cut out the centre of the bread.

3 Lightly oil a frying pan large enough to take the pieces of bread. Heat over a moderate heat, then swirl in a good knob of butter.

4 When the butter starts sizzling, put the hollowed out bread slices in the pan. Carefully break an egg into each central area. Cook over a low heat until the eggs are set, basting the eggs with the hot butter if necessary.

5 Add the 2 circles of bread to the pan. After one minute, turn over the circles of bread. Remove them from the pan after a further minute and reserve.

6 Using a fish slice, carefully position the cooked eggs and their toasted containers on warmed plates. Top with the fried bread circles. Garnish with tomato wedges, if using, season lightly and serve at once.

Œufs au Plat sur Tartine

ŒUFS EN COCOTTE À L'OSEILLE

Baked Eggs with Sorrel

Œuf en cocotte (œufs en cocotte if you are hungry) can be the most comforting of supper dishes.

I love the sharpness of sorrel tempered by other ingredients in the following recipe, but eggs can be baked in dozens of ways. Replace the sorrel with spinach and use exactly the same method. Try chives or dill with smoked salmon and cream cheese, or use cured ham and Parmesan. Simplest but hard to surpass is fresh tarragon, butter and crème fraîche.

SERVES 4 • UNDER 25 MINUTES

about 55 g/2 oz soft butter
handful of young sorrel leaves, trimmed and snipped
4 tbsp crème fraîche, soured cream or single cream
30 g/1 oz Gruyère or Cheddar cheese, grated
½ tsp ground cumin, coriander or mild curry powder (optional)
4 large eggs
sea salt and freshly ground black pepper

1 Preheat the oven to 180C/350F/gas4 and bring a kettle of water to the boil.

2 Meanwhile, put a knob of butter in a small frying pan or saucepan. Heat gently until melted. Add the sorrel and stir for a minute or two until wilted. Tip out on paper towels and pat dry.

3 Reserve a good knob of butter and divide the rest between 4 small ramekins. Spread until their insides are thoroughly coated.

4 Spread the sorrel over the base of the ramekins. Season lightly with salt and generously with pepper.

5 Add 2 teaspoons of cream to each ramekin. Sprinkle with cheese and season with a touch of spice, if liked.

6 Break an egg into each ramekin. Season lightly and top with a dot of the reserved butter.

7 Line a roasting pan with a few layers of newspaper. Put the ramekins in the tray. Pour in boiling water to come halfway up the sides of the ramekins.

8 Bake for about 10 minutes, until the eggs are set to your liking.

ŒUFS SURPRISE EN BRIOCHE

Eggs Baked in Brioche Cases

Serve on a bed of watercress and lettuce salad, or without the chives on a bed of Épinards en Branche (see page 102).

SERVES 2 • UNDER 30 MINUTES

2 chilled day-old individual (but not miniature) brioches
30 g/1 oz soft butter
30 g/1 oz creamy blue cheese, crumbled
2 small eggs, or 4 quails' eggs
few chives
freshly ground black pepper

1 Preheat a baking sheet in the oven to 190C/375F/gas5.

2 Cut off the top from each brioche and reserve. Using a small sharp knife or teaspoon, scoop out the centre (use the crumbs in another recipe).

3 Using a teaspoon, put a small knob of butter in each cavity, then add a little cheese. Carefully break an egg (or 2 quails' eggs) into each and season with pepper.

4 Top each with half of the rest of the butter and cheese.

5 Place on the hot baking sheet and bake for about 15 minutes, until the cheese has melted and the eggs are just set. Add the reserved brioche tops to the baking sheet after 10 minutes.

6 Snip a few chives over the filled brioches and replace the tops before serving.

OMELETTE PAYSANNE

Country-style Folded Omelette

Allow the filling to overflow just a little on the plate and spoon any extra filling on top of the omelette.

SERVES 2 • UNDER 25 MINUTES

4 eggs
1 tbsp milk
cayenne pepper
2 tsp oil
45 g/1½ oz unsalted butter, plus extra if needed
sea salt and freshly ground black pepper

FOR THE FILLING
1 tsp oil
15 g/½ oz butter
1 slice of ham, rolled and snipped into strips
1 large spring onion, snipped
few lettuce leaves, rolled and snipped into strips
1 small tomato, deseeded and chopped (optional)
2 tbsp grated Gruyère or Cheddar cheese

1 First prepare the filling: in a small sauté pan, heat the oil and add the butter. When melted, sauté all the ingredients except the cheese over a moderate heat until hot. Stir in the cheese, season lightly and keep hot.

2 Now make the omelette: whisk the eggs briskly with the milk and season with a touch of cayenne. Heat the oil in a medium-sized frying pan. Then swirl in the butter, reserving a small piece. When it starts to foam and before it turns brown, tip in the eggs.

3 Cook the eggs over a moderate heat, pushing the edges of the mixture towards the centre with a palette knife or heatproof spatula as soon as they begin to set.

4 As soon as the mixture looks set but still moist, slide the palette knife or spatula sideways under the omelette, adding extra butter if necessary. Tilt the pan and slide the omelette sideways to the right in the pan.

5 Spoon the hot filling over the left half of the omelette. Fold the right half over the filling. Slide the omelette on to a warmed plate. Trail the reserved butter over the top, season lightly and serve.

OVERLEAF
Omelette Paysanne

CLAFOUTIS AU GRUYÈRE

Cheese and Bacon Flan

My sister Françoise, who likes her food but prefers to restrict her activity in the kitchen to short sharp bursts, introduced me to this great easy savoury flan. A sort of pastry-less quiche Lorraine, it conveniently keeps well and isn't half bad cold the next day.

SERVES 4 • UNDER 45 MINUTES

1 tsp oil
170 g/6 oz lardons (see page 61) or diced smoked
  bacon
3 spring onions
2 slices of smoked ham, fat removed, rolled into a
  cylinder and snipped across into strips
3 very fresh large eggs
400 ml/14 fl oz full-fat milk
½ tsp dried thyme
pinch each of dried oregano and sage
85 g/3 oz flour
140 g/5 oz grated Gruyère or Cheddar cheese
butter, for greasing
few sprigs of fresh parsley
freshly ground black pepper

1 Preheat a baking sheet in the oven to 220C/425F/gas7.

2 Heat the oil in a frying pan. Add the lardons or bacon, reduce the heat a little and sauté for 2 minutes. Snip in the spring onions. Stir in the ham and season generously with pepper. Reduce the heat to low.

3 Generously butter a 24 cm/9½ in flan dish. Beat the eggs in a bowl until frothy. Pour in the milk and beat again. Sprinkle in the dried herbs, sift in the flour and beat until well combined. Stir in the cheese and season again lightly with pepper.

4 Spread the bacon mixture evenly over the buttered flan dish. Season lightly with pepper and snip over the fresh parsley. Pour in the cheese custard.

5 Bake on the hot baking sheet in the oven for 30-35 minutes, until just set and golden. Check after about 20 minutes and turn down the heat a little if the top of the custard is browning too fast. Leave to settle in the oven with the door open for a few minutes. Serve warm.

CLAFOUTIS AUX ÉPINARDS

Savoury Spinach Flan

Lightly cooked courgette slices (blanched, drained and sautéed) or asparagus (see page 28) can be used instead of spinach in this dish. I sometimes also replace the ham with shredded smoked fish.

SERVES 4 • UNDER 45 MINUTES

1 tsp oil
15 g/½ oz butter, plus extra for greasing
about 350 g/12 oz young leaf spinach, trimmed,
    rinsed and shredded
2 thin slices of dry-cured ham, rolled into a cylinder
    and snipped across into strips (optional)
small pinch of freshly grated nutmeg
3 large eggs
350 ml/12 fl oz full-fat milk
3 tbsp crème fraîche
85 g/3 oz flour
100 g/3½ oz grated Gruyère or Cheddar cheese
salt and freshly ground black pepper

1 Preheat a baking sheet in the oven to 220C/ 425F/gas7.

2 Heat the oil in a frying pan. Add the butter and melt it over a moderate heat. Add the spinach, turn up the heat a little and sauté it for 2-3 minutes, stirring a few times. Generously butter a 24 cm/9½ in flan dish.

3 Stir the ham into the spinach, if using. Season with a small pinch of nutmeg, a touch of salt and a good grinding of pepper. Remove from the heat.

4 Beat the eggs in a bowl until frothy, pour in the milk and beat again. Beat in the cream, then sift in the flour and stir vigorously until well combined. Add the cheese and stir it in lightly. Season again with a little salt and more liberally with pepper.

5 Spread the spinach evenly over the base of the flan dish, then pour in the cheese custard.

6 Cook in the oven on the hot baking sheet for 30-35 minutes, until just set and golden. Check after about 20 minutes and turn down the heat a little if the top of the custard is browning too fast.

7 Leave to settle in the oven with the door open for a few minutes. Serve warm rather than piping hot.

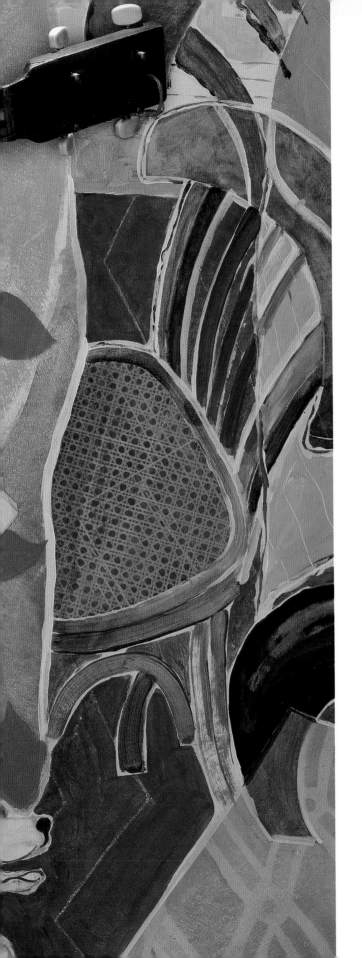

PETITS SNACKS
et
PLATS LÉGERS

Contrary to popular belief, not every French citizen solemnly sits down each day to a substantial two-hour lunch. Light one-course meals are gaining ground on the old structured menu.

CROISSANTS MONSIEUR

Gruyère and Ham Croissants

Thank heaven for croissants. For the cook in a hurry, they are real horns of plenty. This blue cheese filling was suggested by a pâtissière in Clermont-Ferrand I was congratulating on the melt-in-the-mouth light texture of her croissants. We had stopped en route for a late breakfast. The café had run out of croissants and had directed me to the boulangerie-pâtisserie across the road. Much too good just to dip into coffee, I said when I went back for seconds. Try filling them with Fourme d'Ambert and grilling for a few minutes, she replied.

If you find your local croissants disappointing, buy a cylinder of chilled Pillsbury croissant dough. Spoon the filling into the centre and follow the instructions on the wrapping. You will only need half the amount of filling and should allow an extra 20 minutes' baking time.

This version of the famed croque-monsieur never fails to satisfy. To make Croissants Madame, leave the croissants open and top with a fried or poached egg.

SERVES 2 • UNDER 20 MINUTES

2 large fresh croissants
2 thin slices of cooked ham, rolled into a cylinder and snipped across into strips
85 g/3 oz Gruyère cheese, grated
pinch of freshly grated nutmeg
15 g/½ oz butter
freshly ground black pepper

1 Preheat the grill. Carefully halve the croissants lengthwise, leaving the two sides just attached in the centre.

2 Arrange the ham strips over the open croissants. Top with a generous sprinkling of Gruyère, reserving a little to finish. Season with a little nutmeg and pepper.

3 Grill under a moderate heat for 3-5 minutes, until the cheese melts and bubbles.

4 Reduce the heat. Carefully close up each croissant. Sprinkle with the rest of the cheese, dot with butter and grill for 2 more minutes.

Croissants à la Fourme d'Ambert avec Salade Chiffonnade

CROISSANTS À LA FOURME D'AMBERT AVEC SALADE CHIFFONNADE

Blue Cheese Croissants with Mixed Salad

SERVES 4 • UNDER 20 MINUTES

4 large fresh croissants
100 g/3½ oz Fourme d'Ambert or strong ripe blue cheese
2 tbsp Greek-style yogurt
1 tbsp Madeira or sweet wine

FOR THE SALADE CHIFFONNADE
1 scant tbsp walnut oil
1 scant tbsp groundnut or sunflower oil
2 tsp lemon juice
1 small soft lettuce
handful of rocket leaves
small handful of fresh walnut kernels
sea salt and freshly ground black pepper

1 Preheat the grill. Carefully halve the croissants lengthwise, leaving the two sides just attached in the centre.

2 Crumble the cheese into the food processor. Whizz for 2 seconds, then add the yogurt and Madeira or wine and whizz again until just smooth.

3 Using a spatula, spread the mixture over the two halves of each croissant. Grill open for 2-3 minutes until the topping just bubbles.

4 Close up each croissant. Reduce the heat and grill until hot all through.

5 Meanwhile, prepare the Salade Chiffonnade: put the oils into a bowl with the lemon juice. Season lightly with salt and pepper and stir to combine.

6 Roll up the lettuce leaves a few at a time into cigar shapes and cut or snip these across into thin strips. Tip into the bowl together with the rocket leaves and toss until lightly coated.

7 Sprinkle the walnuts with a little salt and dry-fry in a small frying-pan over a moderate heat for a minute or two.

8 Arrange a croissant with some salad on each of 4 plates. Sprinkle with a few walnut kernels and serve hot.

UNE COMMISSION
POUR CHATOU

(Scène véridique. Verzuil 1917)

C'était un beau, un très beau train de permission,
naïves qui s'en allait, tout doucement, trop doucement,
vers l'arrière.

33

TARTINES DE CHARCUTERIE

Open Cold Meat Sandwiches

France's answer to open sandwiches, tartines *are the most genuinely French of all snacks. At its most basic, a* tartine *is a buttered slice of bread – standard breakfast and mid-afternoon fare for generations of French schoolchildren. A touch of jam, honey or – these days – nutty chocolate spread is an optional extra.*

For more grown-up palates, a tartine of pain de campagne (rough-textured country bread) – preferably from Monsieur Poilâne's celebrated bakeries – makes a perfect accompaniment to a wine-tasting session. Spread the slices of bread with pale unsalted Normandy butter and serve with a selection of charcuterie, *such as ultra thin slices of* rosette de Lyon *salami; small slices of saucisse sèche (dried mountain sausage), slivers of jambon de Bayonne and pickled baby gherkins.*

The only real work involved is selecting the wine (definitely red, probably from South-west France, perhaps a Pécharmant or a good Cahors) and persuading the person behind the deli counter to let you taste slivers of saucisson before you buy. Ask for the charcuterie to be cut into very thin slices. All you now have to do is bring the butter to room temperature before you spread your tartines, while you spend a few virtuous minutes skinning the salami . . .

TARTINES PROVENÇALES

Onion and Tomato Toasts

SERVES 4 • UNDER 15 MINUTES

4 tbsp extra virgin olive oil
4 large spring onions, both white and green parts, chopped or snipped
1 garlic clove, crushed
4 slices of country bread
1 large ripe tomato, blanched and skinned
6 black olives, stoned and halved
4 anchovy fillets, drained (optional)
2-3 basil leaves
sea salt and freshly ground black pepper

1 Preheat the grill to high. In a small frying pan, heat 1 tablespoon of olive oil. Add the spring onions and garlic to the pan and sauté over a moderate heat for 2-3 minutes until softened, stirring occasionally.

2 Brush one side of the bread with a little of the remaining olive oil. Thinly slice the tomato, removing the seeds and excess pulp if you wish.

3 Spread the spring onion mixture over the bread and arrange the tomato slices over the top.

4 Top each slice of bread with 3 olive halves and an anchovy fillet, if using. Snip over a little basil, season lightly and sprinkle with the rest of the olive oil.

5 Grill for a few minutes until bubbling hot and serve hot or warm with the remaining basil snipped over.

BAGUETTE AU BRIE FONDU

Melted Brie Toast

This is not exactly an exhausting snack to prepare, but the combination of melting Brie and crushed green peppercorns is irresistible. If you want to turn this into knockout party canapés, cut the baguette crosswise into small slices and be generous with the topping on these.

SERVES 2 • UNDER 15 MINUTES

1 scant tsp green peppercorns
about 30 g/1 oz soft butter
1 small fresh baguette, halved lengthwise
about 75 g/2½ oz ripe Brie at room temperature, rind removed
Salade Chiffonnade (page 48), to serve (optional)

1 Preheat the grill to high.

2 Mash together the green peppercorns and the butter. Spread this evenly over the bread.

3 Halve the Brie, then cut it into slivers and spread it over the flavoured butter.

4 Grill under a moderate heat for a few minutes, until the cheese is melting and bubbling.

5 Serve hot with Salade Chiffonnade, if using.

CROÛTES AUX CHAMPIGNONS

Creamed Mushrooms on Brioche Toasts

SERVES 4 • UNDER 25 MINUTES

1 tsp oil
30 g/1 oz butter
350 g/12 oz mixed mushrooms, sliced or coarsely chopped
4 thick slices of slightly stale brioche
small bunch of chives
mushroom ketchup
2 generous tbsp cream cheese, thick cream or fromage frais
1 tbsp fortified wine such as sherry, port or Madeira
sea salt and freshly ground black pepper

1 Heat the oil with half the butter in a frying pan. Preheat the grill to high.

2 Tip in the mushrooms and sauté for 2-3 minutes over a moderate heat, stirring frequently. Season lightly, add the rest of the butter and sauté for another 3-5 minutes.

3 Lightly toast the brioche slices.

4 Put the sautéed mushrooms in the food processor. Snip in a few chives, add a few drops of mushroom ketchup, the cheese or cream and the fortified wine. Season lightly and whizz for a few seconds, until just a little creamy but still coarse in texture.

5 Spread the mixture over the lightly toasted brioche slices.

6 Grill for a few minutes until piping hot. Snip over a few more chives before serving.

OVERLEAF
LEFT *Tartines de Charcuterie*
RIGHT *Tartines Provençales*

TARTE À LA TOMATE

Tomato Tart

SERVES 4 • UNDER 45 MINUTES

30 g/1 oz butter, plus extra for greasing
One 24 cm/9½ in square of ready-rolled chilled puff
  pastry
1 large egg
1 generous tbsp cream cheese or fromage frais
30 g/1 oz Gruyère or Cheddar cheese, grated
1 tsp Dijon mustard
several sprigs of fresh herbs, such as flat leaf parsley,
  thyme, chervil, savory, marjoram, sage, finely
  snipped, or several pinches of dried herbs
2 fresh ripe tomatoes, blanched and skinned
225 g/8 oz canned chopped tomatoes, well drained
15 g/½ oz freshly grated Parmesan cheese
salt and freshly ground black pepper
flour, for dusting

1 Preheat the oven to 220C/425F/gas7. Butter and flour
a 24 cm/9½ in square in the centre of a baking sheet
and place the pastry on it. Turn up the edge to make a
rim and slit this with a knife at regular intervals.

2 In a bowl, lightly whisk the egg. Remove 1 tablespoon
of it and put this in a saucer. Add a few drops of water
to the saucer and brush this egg and water mixture
lightly over the pastry rim.

3 Return any remaining egg and water to the bowl.
Whisk in the cream cheese or fromage frais, the grated
Gruyère or Cheddar, the mustard and herbs. Season
generously.

4 Thinly slice the fresh tomatoes, discarding seeds and
excess pulp if you wish.

5 Stir the drained canned tomatoes into the seasoned
egg and cheese mixture. Spoon the mixture over the
pastry, spreading it evenly. Arrange the tomato slices on
top. Sprinkle with Parmesan and a little extra pepper.
Dot with butter.

6 Bake for 20-30 minutes, until golden and cooked
through. Check after 15-20 minutes: if the topping is
browning too fast, cover loosely with lightly crushed foil.
With a spatula, check that the pastry base is crisp
enough before removing from the oven.

7 Serve warm rather than piping hot.

SALADE CAMPAGNARDE

Cooked Vegetable Salad with Ham and Cheese

SERVES 4 • UNDER 30 MINUTES

150 g/5½ oz baby new potatoes, well scrubbed
350 g/12 oz sachet of mixed prepared vegetables:
  such as carrot, cauliflower and broccoli
75 g/2½ oz mixed salad leaves
several sprigs of flat leaf parsley
55 g/2 oz smoked or dry-cured ham, rolled into a
  cylinder and snipped across into shreds
85 g/3 oz Gruyère cheese, cut into dice or slivers
6 small spring onions, trimmed

FOR THE DRESSING
3 tbsp good-quality ready-made mayonnaise
1 tbsp fromage frais
2 tsp Dijon mustard
1½ tbsp oil
2 tsp wine vinegar
1 shallot, very finely chopped
sea salt and freshly ground black pepper

1 Bring a kettle of water to the boil. Boil the potatoes in
lightly salted boiling water. After 8-10 minutes, add the
mixed vegetables and cook until they are just tender.

2 While the vegetables are cooking, make the dressing:
combine the ingredients in a bowl until well mixed.
Season to taste.

3 Drain the potatoes and vegetables, refresh under cold
running water and drain well again. Pat dry and toss in
the dressing until well coated.

4 Arrange the mixed salad leaves in a shallow bowl or
suitable dish. Snip over a few sprigs of parsley. Scatter
half the ham and cheese over the salad and season
lightly.

5 Lightly toss the rest of the ham and cheese in the
cooked vegetable mixture. Spoon this into the centre of
the dish. Tuck in the spring onions and snip over a few
more sprigs of parsley.

Tarte à la Tomate

SALADE NICOISE

Tuna, Bean and Tomato Salad

SERVES 4 • UNDER 30 MINUTES

2 eggs
200 g/7 oz baby new potatoes, well scrubbed
200 g/7 oz small French beans, topped and tailed
1 garlic clove, halved
6 tbsp extra virgin olive oil
1 tbsp red wine vinegar
1 oak leaf lettuce, large leaves torn
white parts of 3 large spring onions, thinly sliced
3 ripe tomatoes, thinly sliced, deseeded and excess pulp removed if wished
225 g/8 oz canned tuna in oil, drained and flaked
about 12 black olives
½ tbsp lemon juice
sea salt and freshly ground black pepper

1 Bring a kettle of water to the boil. Hard-boil the eggs for 8-10 minutes in a small pan. In a separate saucepan, boil the potatoes in lightly salted water. After about 12 minutes, add the beans and cook until just done (4-8 minutes depending on the beans). Drain well. Shell the eggs and cut them into wedges.

2 Meanwhile, rub the inside of an attractive shallow bowl or suitable dish with the cut side of the garlic.

3 In a large bowl, beat together the oil and vinegar and season generously.

4 Put the salad leaves in the bowl. Sprinkle with a little dressing, toss lightly and arrange. Then arrange the spring onion and tomato slices on top and sprinkle with a little more dressing.

5 Lightly toss the beans and potatoes in some of the remaining dressing and distribute over the salad. Scatter the tuna on top and tuck in the egg wedges and olives. Season lightly with salt and pepper.

6 Add the lemon juice to what remains of the dressing and sprinkle this over the salad.

SALADE SCANDINAVE

Smoked Fish Salad

SERVES 4 • UNDER 25 MINUTES

½ cucumber, thinly sliced
85 g/3 oz attractive mixed leaves
3 small ripe tomatoes, quartered, deseeded and excess pulp removed if wished
250 g/8½ oz assorted smoked and pickled fish and seafood (such as mackerel, trout, salmon, herrings and mussels), well drained on paper towels and with the fish cut into strips or shreds
sea salt and freshly ground black pepper

FOR THE SAUCE
100 ml/3½ fl oz crème fraîche or soured cream, or a mixture of yogurt and fromage frais
1 tbsp lemon juice, plus extra for sprinkling
1 tbsp mild mustard
1 tbsp oil
1 tbsp wine vinegar
grated or creamed horseradish
small handful of chives

1 Put the cucumber slices in a colander and sprinkle lightly with salt. Cover with a plate, place a weight on top and leave to stand.

2 Make the sauce: combine the cream or yogurt mixture, lemon juice, mustard, oil and vinegar. Taste the horseradish and add just enough to hot up the seasoning – the strength varies. Season with a little salt and plenty of pepper. Snip in several of the chives.

3 Arrange a layer of the mixed leaves in a serving dish. Distribute the tomato wedges on top and snip over some more chives.

4 Lightly toss the fish and seafood in the cream sauce and spoon it on top of the salad.

5 Rinse and drain the cucumber. Press dry firmly with paper towels and arrange attractively over the salad. Season with a little extra pepper and lemon juice. Snip over a few more chives.

SALADE TIÈDE À LA LOTTE

Warm Monkfish Salad

This salad also works well with skate (allow 10 minutes for the fish to become easy to flake with a fork) or salmon fillets (allow about 6-8 minutes).

SERVES 2 • UNDER 30 MINUTES

½ good fish stock cube or court bouillon sachet (see page 13)
about 350 g/12 oz monkfish tail
6 tbsp hazelnut oil, grapeseed oil or light olive oil
1 tbsp raspberry or balsamic vinegar
1 generous tbsp drained capers
about 100 g/3½ oz mixed salad leaves
few fresh coriander leaves
sea salt and freshly ground black pepper

1 Bring a kettle of water to the boil.

2 Pour about 5 cm/2 in of the boiling water into a sauté pan (enough to cover the fish) and dissolve the stock cube or sachet mixture over a moderate heat.

3 Reduce the heat and poach the fish in the gently simmering stock for 3-5 minutes, until just firm.

4 Meanwhile, combine the oil, vinegar and capers in a bowl. Season to taste.

5 Drain the fish well and cut into bite-sized pieces.

6 Toss the salad leaves in two-thirds of the dressing and arrange in a dish.

7 Lightly toss the fish in the rest of the dressing and scatter it over the salad. Sprinkle sparingly with coriander leaves. Serve as soon as possible.

CREVETTES ET CHAMPIGNONS AU BEURRE BRETON

Prawns and Mushrooms with Savoury Butter

I like to serve this little starter in scallop shells. If more convenient for a dinner party, prepare ahead up to the end of step 5 and finish in a couple of minutes just before serving.

SERVES 2-3 • UNDER 25 MINUTES

1 tbsp oil
250 g/8½ oz brown-cap mushrooms, sliced
45 g/1½ oz soft butter
1 small shallot, finely chopped
1 garlic clove, crushed
cayenne pepper
pinch of freshly grated nutmeg
1 tbsp dry white wine
125 g/4½ oz large cooked shelled prawns
few sprigs of flat leaf parsley
sea salt and freshly ground black pepper

1 Heat the oil in a frying pan over a moderate heat. Add the mushrooms, season lightly and sauté for about 5 minutes until just cooked, stirring occasionally.

2 Lift the mushrooms out of the pan with a slotted spoon. Drain on paper towels.

3 Wipe the pan clean with a wad of paper towels.

4 Add the butter to the pan. Swirl over a moderate heat until melted. Sprinkle in the shallot and garlic, reduce the heat a little and stir for a minute or two.

5 Season sparingly with cayenne and nutmeg. Add the wine and stir for a few seconds.

6 Pat the prawns dry with paper towels. Tip them and the mushrooms into the pan and heat through.

7 Snip in the parsley, stir well and serve hot.

OVERLEAF
LEFT *Crevettes et Champignons au Beurre Breton*
RIGHT *Salade Tiède à la Lotte*

PETITE CHOUCROUTE

Quick Sauerkraut with Mixed Meats

Inspired by the menus of countless brasseries alsaciennes, this an easy home version of the celebrated dish. The chicken breast is a personal preference and can be replaced by a more orthodox piece of gammon. If I am cooking this dish for two and there is room in the sauté pan, I halve the larger of the baby potatoes and cook them all in the simmering wine under the sauerkraut. This dish calls for an Alsatian wine, Riesling or Pinot Gris.

SERVES 4 • UNDER 35 MINUTES

1 tbsp oil
1 large sweet white onion, or the white parts of 4
   large spring onions, chopped
100 g/3½ oz thick-cut smoked bacon, diced
200 ml/7 fl oz dry or medium dry white wine
1 scant tsp juniper berries
1 tsp green or black peppercorns
450 g/1 lb good-quality bought sauerkraut
2 small boneless chicken breasts, skinned
4 good-quality frankfurters or Strasbourg sausages
30 g/1 oz butter
115 g/4 oz smoked loin of pork or other smoked
   ham, thinly sliced
freshly ground black pepper

TO SERVE
450 g/1 lb scrubbed baby new potatoes, boiled
Dijon mustard

1 Heat the oil in a large sauté pan. Sauté the onion(s) for 2-3 minutes over a moderate heat, stirring frequently.

2 Add the bacon and sauté for 2 minutes, still stirring.

3 Add the wine, juniper berries and peppercorns. Bring to a simmer and spread one-third of the sauerkraut over the pan.

4 Cut each chicken breast in half lengthwise and put the pieces side by side on the sauerkraut. Top with the rest of the sauerkraut, cover and simmer for 5-8 minutes.

5 Add the sausages, tucking them well into the sauerkraut. Season lightly with pepper, cover and simmer for 5 minutes.

6 Dot with butter and spread the pork slices on top of the dish. Cover and simmer for 3 minutes, until heated through.

7 Rearrange the cooked meats attractively in the centre of the pan. Serve piping hot from the pan, with boiled potatoes and mustard.

BROCHETTES DE FOIE DE VOLAILLE AU BACON

Chicken Liver Kebabs

Serve with lightly dressed mixed salad leaves for a classic salade tiède.

SERVES 4 • UNDER 30 MINUTES

45 g/1½ oz butter
several sprigs of fresh thyme
½ tbsp dried sage
450 g/1 lb fresh chicken livers
12 very thin slices of rindless smoky bacon
sea salt and freshly ground black pepper

1 Preheat the grill to high.

2 In a frying pan, melt the butter over a moderate heat. Snip in the thyme and add the sage. Cook gently for a few minutes, stirring frequently.

3 Add the chicken livers, season lightly and sauté until they are just seized.

4 Wrap the livers in bacon and thread on dampened wooden skewers. Grill for 4-5 minutes, until the bacon is golden, turning the skewers over once during cooking.

FRISÉE AUX LARDONS

Curly Endive and Bacon Salad

With Salade Niçoise (page 56), frisée aux lardons is the most authentically French salade composée. While genuine lardons (succulent cubes of smoked pork belly) are still hard to find outside France, many supermarkets now sell diced bacon – a less fatty and very satisfactory alternative. Diced avocado and garlic croutons are optional extras.

Curly endive is the classic leaf for this salad but if, like me, you find the curls a bit aggressive to chew on, try escarole, lamb's lettuce or shredded raw red or green cabbage. What really matters is eating the salad the moment the sizzling bacon leaves the pan.

Use the same method with fresh chicken livers, cut on the slant and gently sautéed.

SERVES 2 • UNDER 15 MINUTES

115 g/4 oz curly endive leaves
1½ tbsp sunflower oil
100 g/3½ oz diced bacon
1 tbsp red wine vinegar
sea salt and freshly ground black pepper

1 Put the leaves in a shallow bowl. Sprinkle with ½ tablespoon of oil and season lightly with salt and more generously with pepper.

2 Heat the rest of the oil in a frying pan. Add the bacon and sauté over fairly high heat for a few minutes until crisp and golden.

3 Add the vinegar and stir to mix. Tip the contents of the pan over the salad, toss lightly and serve immediately.

SALADE AU ROQUEFORT

Blue Cheese and Oak Leaf Salad

This salad is a firm favourite among my family and friends, whatever their age – even reluctant leaf-eaters. By popular demand a soft-boiled egg (see Baguette Panachée on page 62) is often added to the dressing. Serve in a shallow dish rather than a deep salad bowl.

SERVES 2 • UNDER 15 MINUTES

45 g/1½ oz Roquefort or Fourme d'Ambert cheese, crumbled
1 tbsp fromage frais or cream cheese
1 tbsp Greek-style yogurt or crème fraîche
2 tsp groundnut or sunflower oil
few drops of Tabasco sauce
2 tsp balsamic or white wine vinegar
1 tsp brandy (optional)
115 g/4 oz mixed salad leaves including plenty of oak leaf lettuce
sea salt and freshly ground black pepper

1 Mash the blue cheese with a fork. Combine it with the fromage frais or cream cheese, the yogurt or crème fraîche, the oil, Tabasco, vinegar and brandy (if using).

2 Taste and season lightly with salt and generously with pepper.

3 In a shallow bowl combine the salad and the blue cheese dressing, tossing lightly until the leaves are well coated. Serve immediately.

BAGUETTE PANACHÉE

Salad-filled Baguette

SERVES 2 • UNDER 15 MINUTES

1 large egg
2 tbsp sunflower or light olive oil, plus extra for
   brushing
1½ tsp white wine vinegar
1 scant tsp Dijon mustard
85 g/3 oz mixed salad leaves
1 small very fresh baguette, cut across in half
few sprigs each of chives and flat leaf parsley
sea salt and freshly ground black pepper

1 Put the egg in a small saucepan with enough water to
cover and bring to the boil. Allow to boil for 2 minutes
only.

2 In a large bowl, combine the oil, vinegar and
mustard. Using a teaspoon, scoop out the soft-boiled
egg and mash well into this dressing. Season to taste.

3 Tip in the salad leaves and toss well.

4 Split the pieces of bread lengthwise and brush the
insides lightly with oil. Season with a little pepper.
Spoon the salad over the bread, snip over a little parsley
and chives. Sandwich the pieces of bread back together
again loosely.

LEFT *Salade au Roquefort (page 61)*
TOP RIGHT *Baguette Panachée*
BOTTOM RIGHT *Frisée aux Lardons (page 61)*

POISSONS
et
FRUITS DE MER

Wet and slippery fish can be a bit intimidating, but – if good and fresh – their full flavours and fine textures can be most rewarding.

SAINT-JACQUES AU BEURRE BLANC

Scallops in White Butter

SERVES 2 • UNDER 25 MINUTES

150 ml/¼ pt dry white wine
2 large fresh shallots
few black peppercorns
small bunch of mixed fresh herbs, such as parsley,
    chervil, chives and tarragon
central core of l stalk of lemon grass, snipped, or 2
    thin strips of zest from an unwaxed lemon
2 tbsp white wine vinegar
75 g/2½ oz chilled unsalted butter
4-6 fresh scallops, cleaned and shelled
sea salt and freshly ground black pepper

1 Bring a kettle of water to the boil. In a heavy pan, put
together the wine, half a shallot, the peppercorns and
herbs – reserving a few tiny sprigs for garnish. Add
about 5 cm/2 in of the boiling water and bring back to
the boil. Season lightly. Simmer for a few minutes.

2 Start the beurre blanc: very finely chop the rest of the
shallots. Combine these with the vinegar in a small
saucepan and simmer over a moderate heat until soft
and syrupy. Cut the chilled butter into small dice.

3 Separate the orange coral from the white flesh of the
scallops. Cut the flesh across their depth into 2 discs if
the scallops are large. Reduce the heat under the stock
pan so that the water barely simmers.

4 Finish the beurre blanc: whisk in the butter, one
piece at a time, lifting the pan off the heat a few times.
Reserve 2 or 3 dice of butter and take the pan off the
heat.

5 Put the white scallop discs in the stock. Poach for 1-2
minutes, then add the corals and continue poaching for
another minute – the water should barely simmer.

6 Lift the scallops and corals out of the liquid with a
slotted spoon and arrange on warmed plates, with the
coral at an attractive angle. Pat dry with paper towels.

7 Return the sauce to the heat. Quickly whisk in the
rest of the butter and stir in 2 or 3 teaspoons of the
cooking liquid. Adjust the seasoning.

8 Pour or spoon the beurre blanc over the scallops. Top
each plate with a tiny herb sprig and serve at once.

SAINT-JACQUES POÊLÉES

Pan-fried Scallops

*Scallops, butter and a frying pan . . . watching the great
Michel Lorain prepare the ultimate version of this dish in
his Joigny kitchen was a highlight of my culinary
education. 'Nothing to it', he said. Well perhaps not, but
flex your wrists, control the heat and watch the clock:
the butter has to be just hazelnut-coloured, not
blackened, and the scallops will toughen if you cook
them too long.*

*Serve the slightly sweet scallops with gently acidic
Épinards en Branche (using a little less butter than in the
recipe on page 102) for a great combination.*

SERVES 2 • UNDER 15 MINUTES

1 garlic clove, halved
2 tsp groundnut oil
4-6 fresh scallops, cleaned and shelled
45 g/1½ oz chilled unsalted butter
cayenne
small bunch of chives (optional)
sea salt and freshly ground black pepper

1 Rub the inside of a frying-pan with the cut sides of
garlic. Swirl in the oil and place over a high heat.

2 Separate the orange coral from the white flesh of the
scallops. Cut the flesh across into 2 discs, if the scallops
are large. Season lightly with salt, pepper and cayenne.

3 Reduce the heat to moderate. Add one-third of the
butter to the pan. Swirl until hot. Before the butter
colours, add the white parts of the scallops and cook for
about 1 minute, stirring once or twice.

4 Add the corals and reduce the heat a little. Turn over
the white parts of the scallops and cook for another
minute or slightly longer. Carefully turn over the corals
after a minute and cook for another 50 seconds or so.
Remove the scallops from the pan and keep warm.

5 Turn up the heat a little. Cut the remaining butter
into pieces and add to the pan. Swirl until melted and
lightly browned – immediately lift the pan off.

6 Dribble the hot butter over the scallops. Season again
and snip over a few chives, if using. Eat at once.

Saint-Jacques Poêlées

SOUPE DE LA MER MAISON

Fish and Prawn Soup

SERVES 4 AS A MAIN COURSE OR 6 AS A STARTER
• UNDER 35 MINUTES

1 tbsp oil
1 large white onion, chopped
1 garlic clove, crushed
1 large waxy potato, peeled and cut into small pieces
1 large carrot, peeled and chopped
bouquet garni of bay leaf, parsley sprigs and thyme
300 ml/½ pt Fish Stock (see page 13)
300 ml/½ pt milk
¼ tsp ground saffron
harissa or Tabasco sauce (optional)
450 g/1 lb mixed skinned fish fillets, such as cod and smoked haddock
100 g/3½ oz frozen garden peas (optional when using as main course)
100 g/3½ oz frozen baby broad beans (optional when using as main course)
100 g/3½ oz peeled cooked prawns
yogurt, cream or Rouille (see page 16), to serve
sea salt and freshly ground black pepper

1 Heat the oil in a large heavy saucepan and sauté the onion and garlic over a moderate heat. Stir the potato into the pan, followed by the carrot.

2 Add the bouquet garni, fish stock, milk and saffron. Season lightly with salt and generously with pepper. Bring to a simmer and cook for 5-7 minutes, stirring occasionally. Adjust the seasoning and add a touch of harissa or a few drops of Tabasco, if using. Skim.

3 Cut the fish into thick strips. Add to the soup and simmer gently for 3 minutes, skimming if necessary.

4 Using a ladle, transfer half the solid contents of the soup into the food processor, together with just enough liquid to cover. Whizz the soup in the food processor briefly until smooth and tip it back into the pan. Stir to mix over a moderate heat.

5 Add the peas and beans, if using, followed by the prawns. Stir for a few minutes, until warmed through.

6 Adjust the seasoning. Serve from the pot or more elegantly in warmed plates, with a swirl of yogurt, cream or rouille and a small parsley sprig to garnish.

FRICASSÉE DE FRUITS DE MER

Seafood Sautéed with Fennel

SERVES 2 • UNDER 25 MINUTES

2 medium fennel bulbs, trimmed but some fronds reserved
3-4 spring onions
2 garlic cloves
2 tbsp extra virgin olive oil
¼ tsp dried fennel seeds
½ tsp dried savory or thyme
225 g/8 oz prepared mixed seafood, well drained
2 tsp Pernod (optional)
2-3 tsp lemon juice
sea salt and freshly ground black pepper

1 Bring half a kettle of water to the boil. Chop the fennel bulbs lengthwise in half, remove the cores and coarsely chop.

2 Pour the boiling water into a sauté pan. Season with a little salt, add the chopped fennel and simmer for 3 minutes. Drain well.

3 Meanwhile, snip the spring onion and crush the garlic.

4 Heat half the oil in the pan. Add the fennel seeds, spring onions and garlic. Sauté over a moderate heat for 2 minutes, stirring a few times.

5 Scatter in the blanched fennel and sprinkle in the dried herbs. Season lightly and cook for 3-5 minutes, stirring occasionally.

6 Spoon into a warmed serving dish and keep hot.

7 Dribble the rest of the oil into the pan and swirl to coat. Turn up the heat a little and tip in the seafood. Sprinkle with Pernod, if using, and the lemon juice, and stir until hot and well coated.

8 Season with some more pepper and spoon this over the fennel mixture. Scatter the reserved fennel fronds over the dish and serve immediately.

MOULES MARINIÈRE

Mussels Steamed with Herbs

This is the mother of all French mussel recipes. Now that cleaned mussels are readily available (at a price, alas), splendid moules marinière *have become a very convenient and fun dish to prepare at home.*

SERVES 2 • UNDER 20 MINUTES

1 tbsp oil
2 shallots, finely chopped
250 ml/8 fl oz dry white wine
½ tsp dried thyme
several sprigs of flat leaf parsley and a few chives
few green or black peppercorns
the central cores of 2 stalks of lemon grass, snipped, or a few fine strips of zest from an unwaxed lemon
1.1 litres/2 pt/2 lb fresh mussels, well scrubbed (discarding any which stay open)
1 generous tbsp crème fraîche or single or soured cream
sea salt and freshly ground black pepper
fresh bread and unsalted butter, to serve

1 Swirl the oil in a large sauté pan. Place over a moderate heat and sauté the shallots for a minute or two.

2 Pour in the wine and throw in most of the herbs, the peppercorns and lemon grass or zest. Turn up the heat, cover and bring to a boil. Throw in the mussels and cover again.

3 Cook the mussels for 4-7 minutes, shaking the pan several times, until the shells open.

4 Lift out the cooked mussels with a slotted spoon and discard any that have not opened. Pile them in two warmed bowls or large soup plates.

5 Stir the cream into the cooking juices and warm through. Adjust the seasoning.

6 Dribble the creamy liquid over the mussels through a small sieve. Snip over the remaining few sprigs of herbs. Serve immediately with bread and butter.

MOULES FARCIES

Stuffed Mussels

SERVES 2 AS A MAIN COURSE OR 4-6 AS AN APPETIZER • UNDER 30 MINUTES

1 tbsp oil
1 shallot, finely chopped
200 ml/7 fl oz dry white wine
few sprigs each of flat leaf parsley and thyme
few green or black peppercorns
1.1 litres/2 pt/2 lb large fat fresh mussels, well scrubbed (discarding any which stay open)

FOR THE STUFFING
1-3 garlic cloves, halved
several sprigs of flat leaf parsley
1-2 sprigs of thyme
1 thin slice of day-old bread, crusts removed
1 tsp grated zest from an unwaxed lemon
1 tsp Dijon mustard
85 g/3 oz soft butter, cut into pieces
1-2 tsp brandy
Worcestershire sauce (optional)
sea salt and freshly ground black pepper

1 Cook the mussels as for Moules Marinière until the shells open.

2 While the mussels are cooking make the stuffing: whizz the garlic, parsley and thyme in the food processor for 2-3 seconds. Tip in the bread and lemon zest. Whizz again very briefly. Add the mustard, butter and brandy. Whizz again until the mixture is puréed and season to taste with salt, pepper and a couple of drops of Worcestershire sauce, if using.

3 Using a slotted spoon, lift out the cooked mussels and discard any that haven't opened. Leave the mussels to cool a little and reserve the cooking juices. Strain them and stir in 2-3 teaspoons to the butter purée.

4 When the mussels are cool enough to handle, snap off and discard the top shells. Preheat the grill to high.

5 Using a small teaspoon, generously spread the butter mixture over each mussel in its half shell. Place them in a flameproof gratin dish and grill under a moderate heat for a few minutes until golden and bubbly.

6 Serve hot, moistened with a little cooking juice, and with plenty of bread.

MOUCLADE

Creamy Saffron Mussel Stew

SERVES 2 • UNDER 25 MINUTES

2 tsp oil
2 shallots, chopped
150 ml/¼ pt dry white wine
several sprigs of flat leaf parsley
pinch each of ground coriander, cumin and paprika
1.1 litres/2 pt/2 lb small fresh mussels, well scrubbed
**   (discarding any which stay open)**
1 garlic clove, crushed
¼ tsp ground saffron
30 g/1 oz butter
2 level tsp cornflour
3-4 tbsp single cream
sea salt and freshly ground black pepper

1 Swirl the oil into a large sauté pan over a moderate heat and sauté half the shallots for a minute or two.

2 Pour in the wine and 100 ml/3½ fl oz water. Throw in a few sprigs of parsley and the spices. Season lightly. Turn up the heat, cover and bring to a boil. Throw in the mussels and cover again. Cook for 3-6 minutes, shaking frequently, until the shells open.

3 While they cook, mash the garlic and remaining shallot with the saffron and butter. Season lightly.

4 Lift out the mussels with a slotted spoon and discard any that haven't opened. Leave until just cool enough to handle. Reserve 6-9 attractive mussels and shell the rest. Keep warm.

5 Pour the cooking liquid into a small jug through a very fine sieve. Rinse out the pan. Over a low heat, melt the flavoured butter in the pan. Sprinkle in the cornflour and stir continuously for a minute.

6 Pour in the strained liquid and whisk for a few minutes until it is just bubbling. Lower the heat and simmer for a minute, then stir in the cream. Reduce the heat again and cook for 2-3 minutes, stirring frequently. Adjust the seasoning and add the mussels.

7 Heat through, snip over a little of the remaining parsley and serve at once in warmed soup plates topped with the reserved mussels in their shells.

LEFT *Moules Farcies (page 69)*
RIGHT *Mouclade*

FILETS DE SOLE NORMANDE

Sole Fillets with Cider Cream

My quick one-pan version of the great dish of Dieppe is less complex and richly infused than the original, but far less calorific and still full of flavour.

SERVES 2 • UNDER 30 MINUTES

30-45 g/1-1½ oz butter
140 g/5 oz button mushrooms, thinly sliced
few sprigs of flat leaf parsley
juice and grated zest of ¼ small unwaxed lemon
100 ml/3½ fl oz dry cider or white wine
100 ml/3½ fl oz Fish Stock (see page 13)
2 large sole fillets, skinned
2 generous tbsp crème fraîche or single cream
55 g/2 oz peeled cooked prawns, well drained
sea salt and freshly ground black pepper

1 Heat half the butter in a sauté pan and scatter the mushrooms over the melted butter. Snip in a few sprigs of parsley, reserving some for garnish if you wish. Add the lemon zest, season lightly and sauté over a moderate heat for a minute or two, stirring a few times.

2 Spread the mushroom mixture evenly in the pan. Pour in the dry cider and stock and bring to a gentle simmer. Reduce the heat a little.

3 Lightly season the sole fillets and place in the pan. Cover the pan and poach them for 3-6 minutes, depending on size and thickness, until just stiff.

4 Lift the fillets out of the pan with a fish slice and place on a warmed serving dish. Turn up the heat to high. Lift the mushrooms out of the pan and distribute them over the sole fillets.

5 Leave the sauce to bubble vigorously until reduced by nearly half. Whisk in the cream and warm through, still whisking. Whisk in half the reserved butter. Pour this sauce over the sole and mushrooms.

6 Wipe the pan clean with a thick wad of paper towels. Swirl the rest of the butter around the pan until melted. Add the prawns, stir over a high heat for a minute, season lightly and sprinkle with the lemon juice.

7 Scatter the sautéed prawns over the contents of the serving dish. If you like, snip over a sprig of parsley and serve at once.

COLIN POÊLÉ AUX CÂPRES

Pan-fried Cod with Caper and Mustard Sauce

As children we used to make faces when pan-fried cod was put in front of us Friday after Friday. Why did I not enjoy it then, when it was inexpensive and cooked for me? Pan-fried cod, served with a little sauce whisked up from the pan juices and a touch of wine, cream etc, is one of the great homely dishes of France. I love it with a gutsy mix of anchovies, capers and mustard, but you may prefer to use the smaller of the quantities listed.

SERVES 2 • UNDER 20 MINUTES

2 cod steaks, each weighing about 170 g/6 oz and
    about 2.5 cm /1 in thick
1 tsp flour
2 tbsp oil, plus extra if necessary
2-3 anchovy fillets, drained and mashed
1-2 tsp capers, drained
about 15 g/½ oz butter, plus extra if necessary
4 tbsp dry white wine
1-2 tsp Dijon mustard
2 tbsp crème fraîche, soured or single cream or
    fromage frais
few sprigs of fresh herbs (optional)
sea salt and freshly ground black pepper

1 Pat the cod dry with paper towels. Season the flour with salt and pepper. Tip it into a small fine sieve and dust the cod with this seasoned flour.

2 Heat half the oil in a frying pan over a moderate heat. Combine the rest of the oil with the anchovy and capers and set aside.

3 Add half the butter to the pan and swirl until melted. Add the fish and cook carefully for 3-4 minutes over a moderate heat. To prevent sticking, slip a fish slice or palette knife under the fish and add a little butter.

4 Turn the steaks over with a fish slice and cook in the same way on the other side. Lift the fish from the pan and keep hot on warmed plates.

5 Turn up the heat a little under the pan. Add the anchovy mixture, stir and then pour in the wine. Bring to a simmer, stirring frequently. Stir in the mustard, then the cream or fromage frais and adjust the seasoning.

6 Stir in the rest of the butter and dribble the sauce over the cod. Snip over fresh herbs, if using, and serve.

SARDINES GRILLÉES AU BASILIC

Grilled Sardines with Basil Sauce

If your sardines are on the small side, start the sauce before grilling. I sometimes replace the lemon and basil with lime and fresh coriander.

SERVES 2 • UNDER 25 MINUTES

2-4 fresh sardines (depending on size), gutted and
   rinsed
about 2 tbsp extra virgin olive oil
1 shallot, finely chopped
1 or 2 garlic cloves, crushed
2 ripe tomatoes, blanched, skinned, deseeded and
   chopped
5 tbsp dry white wine
5 tbsp Fish Stock (see page 13) or water
3-4 stoned black olives, chopped
15 g/½ oz chilled butter
several leaves of fresh basil
sea salt and freshly ground black pepper
½ lemon or lime, cut into 2 wedges, to serve

1 Preheat the grill to high. Generously brush the sardines with some of the olive oil and season lightly.

2 Grill the sardines for 5-10 minutes, depending on size, turning them over once or twice. The cooked sardines should look a little charred on the outside and be just a little flaky inside.

3 Meanwhile, heat a tablespoon of the oil in a small saucepan. Stir the shallot and garlic into the oil and sauté for a minute over a moderate heat. Add a little more oil and the chopped tomatoes. Sauté for a minute, then pour in the wine and stock or water. Bring to a simmer.

4 Simmer for a few minutes, until slightly reduced and thickened. Stir in the olives and warm through. Season to taste.

5 Just before serving, whisk in the butter and snip in the basil. Pour over the sardines and serve with the lemon or lime wedges.

OVERLEAF
LEFT *Sardines Grillées au Basilic*
RIGHT *Sole Meunière*

SOLE MEUNIÈRE

Sautéed Sole with Parsley

I really only got into 'hands-on' fish cooking a few summers ago in Saint-Malo. We were staying in a charming crooked house overlooking the long sandy beach outside the ramparts. Our absent friend's kitchen was that of a good French home cook of the old school – frugal and gadget-free, but thoughtfully equipped. I soon noticed no fewer than three oblong fish pans. So I took the hint, went to the market (literally wet and slippery) and the supermarket (more tame but still pretty fresh-looking) and came back laden with fish and seafood. The time had come to experiment and I cooked fish practically every night. Very educational, but I would not recommend pan-frying, grilling and poaching for 7 people to novice fish cooks without sous chefs – not if they want to sit down and eat with the rest of the gang.

SERVES 2 • UNDER 25 MINUTES

2 lemon or baby Dover soles, cleaned and gutted
about 1 tbsp flour
1 tbsp oil
75 g/2½ oz soft butter
several sprigs of flat leaf parsley
1 unwaxed lemon
sea salt and freshly ground black pepper

1 Season the flour with a little salt and a more generous amount of pepper. Tip into a small fine sieve and lightly dust the prepared soles with this seasoned flour.

2 Heat the oil in a large frying pan over a moderate heat. Swirl in one-third of the butter. When it starts to sizzle, put the sole in the pan and cook for 4-5 minutes.

3 Turn over with a fish slice and continue cooking for 4-5 minutes, adding a little more butter. Turn up the heat just a little for the last minute. Transfer to warmed plates. Wipe the pan with paper towels.

4 Reduce the heat and swirl the rest of the butter in the pan. Snip in a little parsley. Cut the lemon in half, grate 1 teaspoon of zest and extract 1 teaspoon of juice from one half and then thinly slice the other half. Add the lemon juice and zest to the pan and stir until warmed through.

5 Pour the pan juices over the sole. Snip over a little more parsley and season lightly. Serve with the lemon slices.

SAUMON POÊLÉ AU POIVRE VERT

Pan-grilled Salmon Fillets with Green Peppercorns

This green peppercorn sauce is very minimalist, but it is a splendid and painless way to dress top-quality salmon fillets. Serve with either Warm Potato Salad (see page 106) or plainly dressed pasta and Braised Lettuce with Radicchio (see page 107).

SERVES 4 • UNDER 25 MINUTES

4 very fresh salmon fillets with their skins, each weighing about 170 g/6 oz
3 tbsp extra virgin olive oil
85 g/3 oz butter
1 level tbsp drained green peppercorns
1 tbsp lemon juice
sea salt and freshly ground black pepper

1 Brush the skin of each fillet with a teaspoon of olive oil and season lightly with pepper.

2 Grease a sauté pan with half the remaining oil. Put over a fairly high heat and add about half the butter. Swirl the foaming butter around the pan and add the salmon fillets, skin side down.

3 Cook for about 5-7 minutes without turning, keeping an eye on the heat. The skin will char and the salmon flesh should begin to change colour.

4 Brush the rest of the oil over the salmon flesh and season lightly. Cover, reduce the heat a little and cook for another 3-5 minutes, until the salmon is done to your liking but still a little moist.

5 Lift the salmon fillets from the pan with a fish slice and place on warmed plates.

6 Scatter the green peppercorns in the pan, swirl in the rest of the butter and sprinkle in the lemon juice.

7 Dribble the pan contents over the salmon, scraping the pan well to make sure you don't waste any bits and juice.

Filet de Saumon Poché avec Petite Sauce Citronnée

FILET DE SAUMON POCHÉ AVEC PETITE SAUCE CITRONNÉE

Poached Salmon with Quick Lemon Sauce

A mixture of water, wine vinegar and honey infused with strongly flavoured herbs such as dill or tarragon makes a good poaching medium for salmon. For less rich fish, combine the water with a few strips of lemon zest, a bay leaf and some milder herbs such as parsley or chervil. What really matters is keeping the poaching water at a mere simmer. Lift the fish out of the pan as soon as it shows signs of flaking: it will go on cooking for a little while after it is removed from the heat.

SERVES 3 • UNDER 25 MINUTES

about 450 g/1 lb salmon fillets with their skin
few sprigs of mixed fresh herbs (see above)
1 tbsp red or white wine vinegar
1 tsp honey or sugar
salt and freshly ground black pepper
Petite Sauce Citronnée (see page 14), to serve

1 Put just enough water to cover the salmon in a sauté pan together with the herbs, vinegar and honey or sugar. Season well and bring to the boil.

2 As soon as the water bubbles, place the salmon in the pan and reduce the heat. Bring back to a simmer and cook over a low heat for 8-10 minutes, until the flesh just begins to flake a little when pierced with a fork.

3 While the fish is cooking, start making the sauce as described on page 14 using 100 ml/3½ fl oz of the fish cooking liquid, reserving one-third of the butter, the lemon juice and egg yolk.

4 Carefully lift the salmon out of the pan with a fish slice. Drain and place on several layers of paper towels and leave until cool enough to peel off the skin.

5 Finish the sauce: in a cup, combine the egg yolk with the lemon juice and a couple of spoonfuls of the hot sauce. Whisk this egg mixture back into the pan of sauce and continue whisking for a minute.

6 Just before serving, whisk the rest of the butter into the sauce. Adjust the seasoning, adding a little extra lemon juice, if liked. Snip in a little more parsley and lemon zest and serve piping hot in a small bowl.

VIANDES
et
VOLAILLES

*The meat course has remained
the heart of the French meal – the
undisputed* plat principal.

STEAK HACHÉ AUX ANCHOIS

Minced Steak with Anchovy Sauce

SERVES 2 • UNDER 25 MINUTES

2 tsp black peppercorns
2 top-quality hamburgers
½ garlic clove
oil for greasing
sea salt and freshly ground black pepper

FOR THE SAUCE
25 g/¾ oz butter
4 canned anchovy fillets, drained and finely snipped,
   or 1 tbsp good anchovy purée
white part of a large spring onion, finely chopped
100 ml/3½ fl oz red wine
2 tsp brandy
1 tbsp crème fraîche or fromage frais
freshly ground black pepper

1 Using a pestle and mortar, crush the peppercorns. Sprinkle them over the hamburgers, pat in gently and leave for a few minutes.

2 Rub a griddle, grill pan or non-stick frying pan with garlic, brush with a little oil and heat the pan or grill until very hot.

3 Start the sauce: in a small heavy saucepan, melt half the butter. Add the anchovies and spring onion, and cook for a minute over a moderate heat, stirring.

4 Add the red wine and cook for 2-3 minutes until a little reduced, stirring from time to time. Stir in the brandy and 3 tablespoons of water. Continue simmering for a minute, or reduce the heat and simmer very slowly until ready to use.

5 Meanwhile, season the hamburgers with salt and pepper. Grill for 5-7 minutes on each side until done to your liking.

6 Just before serving, stir the crème fraîche or fromage frais into the sauce. Beat in the rest of the butter and season with pepper. Spoon the sauce over and to the side of each hamburger.

Brochettes de Bœuf à la Citronnelle

BROCHETTES DE BŒUF À LA CITRONNELLE

Beef Kebabs with Peppers and Lemon Grass

Ever since I first tasted lemon grass in our local Vietnamese restaurant in Paris, I have been completely hooked on the delicate flavour of citronnelle. Chicken or pork can be used instead of beef for these fragrant brochettes. Serve with rice, bulgur or couscous (see the Introduction on page 13).

SERVES 2 • UNDER 30 MINUTES

115 g/4 oz lean fillet steak
1 small yellow sweet pepper
1 small red sweet pepper
white parts of 4 spring onions

FOR THE COATING
1 tbsp sesame oil
2 tbsp groundnut oil, plus extra for brushing
1 tbsp soy sauce
tender inner parts of 2 lemon grass stalks
harissa or hot chilli sauce
sea salt and freshly ground black pepper

1 Cut the beef into cubes no larger than 4 cm/1½ in.

2 Make the coating: combine the oils and soy sauce. Finely snip the lemon grass. Add to the oil mixture with a pinch of harissa or hot chilli sauce. Adjust the seasoning, if necessary, with a little salt and pepper. Brush this coating over the beef and set aside while you prepare the other ingredients.

3 If you prefer skinned peppers, bring a pan of water to the boil and blanch the peppers for 2-3 minutes. Drain, then peel off the skin when they are cool enough to handle.

4 Preheat the grill to high.

5 Remove the core and seeds of the peppers and cut the flesh into pieces about the same size as the pieces of beef. Trim the spring onions.

6 Thread the beef, peppers and spring onions on 4 dampened wooden skewers. Brush the peppers and onions with a little groundnut oil.

7 Season and grill for 4-5 minutes, turning the kebabs over once, until cooked to your liking.

SAUTÉ DE BŒUF À LA TOMATE

Beef Strips with Green Peppercorns, Tomato and Madeira

Green peppercorns have a fresh pungency that never fails to bring to life even the dullest of ingredients. A little jar of peppercorns in brine is well worth its modest shelf space in the refrigerator. They mix particularly well with that other unsung hero of the French store cupboard, cheap supermarket Madeira. To drink, try a well-made Côtes du Rhône or a Beaujolais.

SERVES 4 • UNDER 25 MINUTES

3 tsp drained green peppercorns
450 g/1 lb lean fillet of beef, cut into strips no longer than 7.5 cm/3 in and about 2.5 cm/1 in wide
1 tbsp oil
4 tbsp Madeira or other good medium-sweet fortified wine
1 tbsp tomato paste
4 tbsp beef or veal stock, or 4 tbsp water with 2 tsp soy sauce and a few drops of mushroom ketchup
15 g/½ oz chilled butter, diced
few leaves of basil (optional)
sea salt

1 Coarsely crush two-thirds of the peppercorns. Sprinkle these over the beef and pat well in. Season lightly with salt.

2 Heat the oil until very hot in a wok or sauté pan. Sauté the meat over a high heat for 2-3 minutes until seized and browned, stirring fairly constantly.

3 Lift the meat from the pan with a slotted spoon and keep it warm on a plate. Tip out any fatty juices from the pan.

4 Reduce the heat a little and pour in the wine. Add the rest of the peppercorns and stir for a few seconds. Add the tomato paste and stir to mix. Add the stock, turn up the heat and bring to a fast simmer. Cook for 2-3 minutes, stirring frequently.

5 Tip in the beef strips and any juices. Reduce the heat and cook for 2-3 minutes. Adjust the seasoning.

6 Just before serving, beat in the butter. If you like, snip in a few fresh basil leaves.

POT AU FEU MINUTE

Beef Fillet Poached with Vegetables

SERVES 4 • UNDER 40 MINUTES

1.1 litres/2 pt beef stock (or 500 ml/1 pt beef stock mixed with 500 ml/1 pt water, 1 tbsp soy sauce and a sprinkling of mushroom ketchup)
200 g/7 oz baby new potatoes, well scrubbed
200 g/7 oz baby turnips, trimmed and peeled or scrubbed
200 g/7 oz baby carrots, trimmed and peeled or scrubbed
2 baby cabbages, quartered
125 g/4½ oz brown-cap mushrooms, wiped and sliced
125 g/4¼ oz mange-tout peas, topped and tailed
450 g/1 lb beef fillet, cut on the slant into large strips
sea salt and freshly ground black pepper

TO SERVE
bowl of Mayonnaise (see page 00), flavoured with extra mustard, snipped herbs and chopped gherkins
small bowl of coarse sea salt mixed with snipped parsley

1 Bring the stock to a simmer in a large saucepan over a high heat. Add the potatoes and turnips, bring back to a simmer and reduce the heat to moderate. Simmer for 5 minutes. Add the carrots and bring back to a simmer. Simmer for 5 minutes.

2 Add the cabbages and mushrooms. Simmer for 5 minutes.

3 Taste the broth and adjust the seasoning with salt and pepper, if necessary. Add the mange-tout and bring back to a simmer.

4 Tuck the beef strips among the vegetables. Reduce the heat a little and simmer very gently for about 5-7 minutes until cooked through; the liquid should barely bubble.

5 Serve heaped in a warmed shallow bowl, moistened with a dribble of cooking liquid. Serve the rest of the liquid in a jug along with the Mayonnaise and herbed salt. Use any remaining liquid as stock.

CASSOULET TGV

Express Bean and Sausage Stew

TGV (Train à Grande Vitesse) is what the French call their high-speed trains. Far be it from me to say that this quick cassoulet *is the real thing, but it is most acceptable and a good dish for a winter mid-week supper party.*

SERVES 6 • UNDER 35 MINUTES

6 Toulouse or other spicy country sausages
250 g/8½ oz goose or duck confit (small can or jar)
200 g/7 oz very thick-cut smoked bacon, chopped
1 Spanish onion, finely chopped
2 large garlic cloves, crushed
450 g/1 lb canned chopped tomatoes
2 bouquets garnis
1 generous tbsp Dijon mustard
several drops of Worcestershire sauce
3 tbsp brandy
about 150 ml/¼ pt strong stock or canned beef
    consommé
about 600 g/1 lb 6 oz canned white haricot beans,
    drained and rinsed
55 g/2 oz day-old breadcrumbs
few sprigs of parsley (optional)
freshly ground black pepper

1 Preheat the grill to high. When very hot, put the sausages under the grill, reduce the heat and grill slowly. Turn from time to time, while you cook the stew. Remove the sausages and keep warm.

2 Heat a large sauté pan or heavy saucepan. Spoon in a little fat from the confit to coat the base. Add the bacon and sauté for a minute. Stir in the onion and garlic and sauté for 3-4 minutes over a moderate heat.

3 Cut the confit into small pieces and add to the pan with a little more fat. Reserve the rest, to finish the dish (any left over can be chilled for use in another dish). Add the tomatoes and their juice, the bouquets garnis, mustard, Worcestershire sauce, brandy and stock. Stir well and simmer gently for at least 15 minutes.

4 Stir in the beans, season with pepper and heat through. Arrange the sausages on top of the dish. Sprinkle with breadcrumbs, snip over a little parsley, if you like, and dot with a little of the reserved goose fat. Grill for 2-3 minutes and serve.

CÔTES D'AGNEAU AU ROMARIN

Grilled Lamb Cutlets with Rosemary Sauce

SERVES 2 • UNDER 30 MINUTES

4 best end of neck lamb cutlets, trimmed
½ garlic clove
lemon pepper or a little finely grated zest from an
    unwaxed lemon
few sprigs of rosemary, fresh or dried
sea salt and freshly ground black pepper
olive oil for greasing

FOR THE SAUCE
1 shallot, finely chopped
1 tsp ground dried rosemary
100 ml/3½ fl oz dry white wine
1 tbsp white wine vinegar
45 g/1½ oz butter
1 scant tsp cornflour
100 ml/3½ fl oz lamb stock or Chicken Stock
    (see page 13)

1 Brush a cast iron griddle or the grill grid with a little olive oil and heat to high. Prepare the cutlets: rub well with garlic and season with pepper and lemon pepper or zest. Press in a little rosemary and leave to stand.

2 Start the sauce: in a small heavy pan, combine the shallot, rosemary, wine and vinegar. Boil until reduced by about two-thirds. Tip into a small cup.

3 Reduce the heat. Melt one-third of the butter, stir in the cornflour and continue stirring for a minute to make a roux. Gradually add the stock and the reduced wine mixture, still stirring vigorously. Season to taste.

4 Bring to a low boil, stirring very frequently, then reduce the heat and simmer for 2-3 minutes, still stirring. Reduce the heat to very low and stir a few times while you cook the cutlets.

5 Season the cutlets and grill over or under a high heat for a few minutes on each side until done to your liking.

6 Stir the rest of the butter and any cooking juices from the pan into the sauce. Adjust the seasoning and dribble the sauce on and around the cutlets.

OVERLEAF
LEFT *Cassoulet TGV*
RIGHT *Pot au Feu Minute*

CÔTES DE PORC AU CIDRE

Pork Chops with Cider

This dish makes good supper fare served with Gratin de Pommes de Terre Express (see page 104), Émincé de Chou (see page 98) and a glass of dry cider.

SERVES 2 • UNDER 30 MINUTES

2 medium pork chops, trimmed
½ tbsp Dijon mustard
pinch each of dried thyme and savory
2 tsp redcurrant or apple jelly
1 tbsp oil
150 ml/¼ pt dry cider
1 tbsp fromage frais
15 g/½ oz chilled butter
sea salt and freshly ground black pepper

1 Slash the fat at regular intervals around the pork. Combine a little salt and pepper with the mustard, herbs and jelly. Coat the chops with this seasoning mixture.

2 Heat the oil in a frying pan or sauté pan over a high heat and seize the pork chops all over until browned, starting by standing them upright on their fatty edges using tongs or two forks.

3 Add the cider to the pan and reduce the heat. Cover and simmer for 15-18 minutes, depending on the thickness of the chops, turning them halfway through cooking. Leave to stand covered for 2 minutes.

4 Lift the chops from the pan and put on warmed plates. Keep warm.

5 Turn up the heat and bring the sauce to a fast simmer, stirring frequently. Cook until reduced by half.

6 Stir in the fromage frais.

7 Just before serving, cut the butter into small pieces and whisk them into the sauce. Pour the sauce over the chops to serve.

ÉMINCÉ DE PORC AUX PRUNEAUX ET À L'ORANGE

Pork Strips with Prunes and Orange

SERVES 4 • UNDER 25 MINUTES

Beer, prunes and mustard are a classic casserole combination. Here they release their flavour quickly over a high heat for the benefit of permeable tender fillet strips. To achieve a 'casserole effect' – a gutsy blend of flavours in minutes (comfortably within half-an-hour) – I tend to rely on the following method.

Cut tender lean meat into small thin pieces. Press in the seasoning and stir over a high heat until well seized and brown. Set aside while you boil up and concentrate the cooking liquid. Dilute a little with fruit juice or water to soften the flavour, return the meat and juices to the pan and simmer gently for a few minutes.

Serve the pork on a bed of buttered small pasta (coquillettes – mini macaroni – are a great French stand-by) with a sprinkling of snipped parsley. Also try Choux de Bruxelles au Carvi (see page 100).

450 g/1 lb lean pork fillet, cut into strips about 2.5 cm/1 in wide and no longer than 7.5 cm/3 in long
finely grated zest and juice of 1 unwaxed orange
1 tbsp oil
150 ml/¼ pt brown ale or bitter
2 tsp light soy sauce
1 tbsp coarse grain mustard
4 pre-soaked stoned prunes, chopped
30 g/1 oz chilled butter, diced
sea salt and freshly ground black pepper

1 Season the pork fillet with a little salt and pepper and with the orange zest. Heat the oil in a wok or large frying pan.

2 Stir-fry the pork over a high heat for 2-3 minutes until seized and browned. Remove from the wok with a slotted spoon and keep warm. Tip out the fatty juices or wipe off with a wad of paper towels.

3 Pour in the beer and bubble over a high heat for 2-3 minutes until reduced, stirring frequently. Add the soy sauce, orange juice, mustard, prunes and 5 tablespoons of water. Reduce the heat a little and cook for about 8 minutes, stirring frequently.

4 Adjust the seasoning. Tip in the pork and simmer gently for 3-4 minutes. Stir in the butter and serve.

PETITE FRICASSÉE DE POULET AU VINAIGRE ET À L'ESTRAGON

Chicken with Tarragon and Vinegar

SERVES 2 • UNDER 35 MINUTES

4 chicken thighs, boned and skinned
1 tsp flour
1 tbsp oil
several sprigs of fresh tarragon
1½ tbsp white wine vinegar
125 ml/4 fl oz Chicken Stock (see page 13) or water
   mixed with 1 tbsp light soy sauce
3 tbsp juice and 2 tsp finely grated zest from an
   unwaxed orange
25 g/¾ oz chilled butter, diced
sea salt and freshly ground black pepper

1 Halve the chicken thighs lengthwise. Season the flour
with a little salt and pepper. Dredge this lightly over the
chicken using a small sieve.

2 Heat the oil in a sauté pan. Sauté the chicken in it
over a moderate heat until evenly coloured.

3 Add the leaves from 4 or 5 tarragon sprigs, sprinkle
with 1 tablespoon of vinegar, and stir well.

4 Stir in the stock and the grated zest. Bring to a
simmer, cover tightly and cook gently for 15-20
minutes, stirring a few times.

5 Lift the chicken from the pan and keep warm.

6 Turn up the heat, bring the liquid to a fast simmer
and reduce slightly for a couple of minutes, stirring from
time to time.

7 Reduce the heat, stir in the rest of the vinegar and the
orange juice.

8 Whisk in the butter and adjust the seasoning. Return
the chicken to the pan and stir to coat. Snip in a few
more tarragon leaves just before serving.

SUPRÊME DE POULET À L'INDIENNE

Chicken Strips in a Light Curry Sauce

À l'indienne *almost invariably refers to dishes spiced
with a mild creamy curry sauce. Plain boiled rice is the
best accompaniment for this dish.*

SERVES 2 • UNDER 30 MINUTES

2 skinned boned chicken breasts, cut into strips
1 tbsp groundnut oil
1 tbsp double cream
sea salt and freshly ground black pepper
3 tbsp Greek-style yogurt, to finish
few leaves of fresh coriander, to garnish

FOR THE COATING
½ tbsp grated peeled fresh root ginger
snipped zest of ½ small unwaxed lemon
few leaves of mint, snipped
1 crushed garlic clove
½ tsp ground coriander
pinch of hot chilli sauce
½ tsp ground cumin
pinch of ground saffron

1 Combine the ingredients for the coating in a bowl.

2 Toss the chicken strips in the coating mixture. Set
aside for a few minutes.

3 Heat the oil in a sauté pan. Sauté the coated strips
over a moderate heat for 3 minutes, stirring frequently.

4 Stir in the rest of the coating mixture and the cream.
Reduce the heat, season and cook for another 3
minutes.

5 Just before serving, stir in the yogurt, adjust the
seasoning and heat through. Then snip over a few fresh
coriander leaves.

POUSSINS GRILLÉS AU CITRON VERT

Grilled Baby Chickens with Lime Glaze

This recipe was inspired by a wonderful chicken dish I ate at the home of a French West-Indian friend.

SERVES 2 • UNDER 45 MINUTES

2 small poussins, each weighing about 300 g/10½ oz
55 g/2 oz soft butter
grated zest and juice of 1 unwaxed lime
2 garlic cloves, well crushed
½ tsp ground coriander
½ tsp dried lemon thyme
¼ tsp harissa or chilli paste
2 tsp runny honey
2 tbsp Greek-style yogurt
sea salt and freshly ground black pepper

1 Preheat the grill to high. Cut the poussins in half lengthwise. You can also help speed the cooking by pressing the halves down with a rolling pin to flatten.

2 Put half the butter in a cup. Season generously then add half the lime zest, the garlic, coriander, lemon thyme and harissa. Mix well to combine.

3 Using a small palette knife or the back of a jam spoon with a long handle, spread the butter mixture in between the skin and the flesh of the birds.

4 Combine the rest of the butter and lime zest with the juice and the honey. Brush over the birds and season.

5 Grill breast-side up for 10 minutes under a high heat, collecting the juices in the grill pan. Turn over and grill for 10 minutes, still under a high heat.

6 Turn the heat down a little and turn the birds back to their original position. Baste with the pan juices and any remaining butter mixture. Continue roasting for 10 minutes or until cooked through (the juices run clear when you pierce the thickest part of the flesh). Leave to rest for a few minutes before serving.

7 Whisk the yogurt into the pan juices and dribble this sauce over the poussins.

TOP *Émincé de Porc aux Pruneaux et à l'Orange (p. 86)*
BOTTOM *Poussins Grillés au Citron Vert*

AIGUILLETTES DE CANARD

Duck Strips with Mushrooms and Tomatoes

SERVES 2 • UNDER 30 MINUTES

1 garlic clove, halved
1 duck breast, trimmed of extra fat, both flesh and
   skin cut into strips
about 5-6 tbsp medium-dry white wine
115 g/4 oz brown-cap mushrooms, sliced
2 ripe tomatoes, blanched, skinned, deseeded and
   chopped
2 spring onions, snipped
3 tbsp Chickens Stock (see page 13) or water
15 g/½ oz butter
sea salt and freshly ground black pepper
oil, for greasing
few sprigs of chervil and parsley, to garnish

1 Lightly grease a frying or sauté pan with oil. Rub the
inside with the cut side of the garlic.

2 Place over a high heat. Add the strips of duck skin
and sauté for a couple of minutes until browned.

3 Reduce the heat a little, then add the strips of flesh.
Season and sauté for a few minutes over a moderate
heat, stirring frequently.

4 Moisten with the wine. Cook until hot and bubbling.

5 Tip the duck and wine out of the pan into a bowl and
reserve.

6 Add the mushrooms, tomatoes and spring onions to
the pan together with 2-3 tablespoons of stock or water.
Cook for a few minutes, then return the duck and liquid
to the pan.

7 Stir in the butter. Season and serve, with chervil and
parsley snipped over.

Petits Choux Farcis

PETITS CHOUX FARCIS

Baby Cabbage Stuffed with Smoked Ham

*Traditional chou farci is a satisfyingly solid dish that takes
a long time to prepare. My quick version will not amuse
purists – but it is stuffed cabbage, it looks and tastes
pretty good and it is far less heavy than its big brother.*

SERVES 4 • UNDER 25 MINUTES

4 baby cabbages, cored
2 tsp oil
85 g/3 oz finely diced or snipped bacon
2 tbsp pine kernels
½ tsp each dried thyme, sage and oregano
3 generous tbsp cream cheese
3 tbsp dry white wine
4 thin slices of dry-cured ham
55 g/2 oz butter
½ tsp caraway seeds
sea salt and freshly ground black pepper

1 Bring to the boil a saucepan of lightly salted water just
large enough to take the 4 cabbages side by side. Place
the cabbages in the boiling water, cover tightly and boil
for 5-7 minutes, until just cooked but still firm.

2 Meanwhile, heat the oil in a small frying pan. Add the
bacon and sauté over a moderate heat for 2-3 minutes,
stirring frequently. Add the pine kernels, the dried
herbs, the cream cheese and white wine and reduce
the heat. Cook for 3-5 minutes, still stirring.

3 Roll up the ham into a cigar shape and snip across
into the pan. Stir, season to taste and heat through.

4 Drain the cabbages, reserving 5-7 tablespoons of the
cooking liquid. Pat dry with a clean tea towel or paper
towels. Leave until just cool enough to handle. Add the
reserved cooking liquid and half the butter to the warm
saucepan and place over a low heat.

5 Gently pull some of the leaves away from the centre
of one of the cabbages and spoon in the stuffing from
the frying pan. Press the leaves back into shape and add
the cabbage to the saucepan. Stuff the other cabbages
in the same way and add to the pan.

6 Dot the top of each cabbage with the rest of the
butter and a few caraway seeds. Cover and heat
through for a few minutes. Spoon the buttery juices
over the cabbages and serve hot.

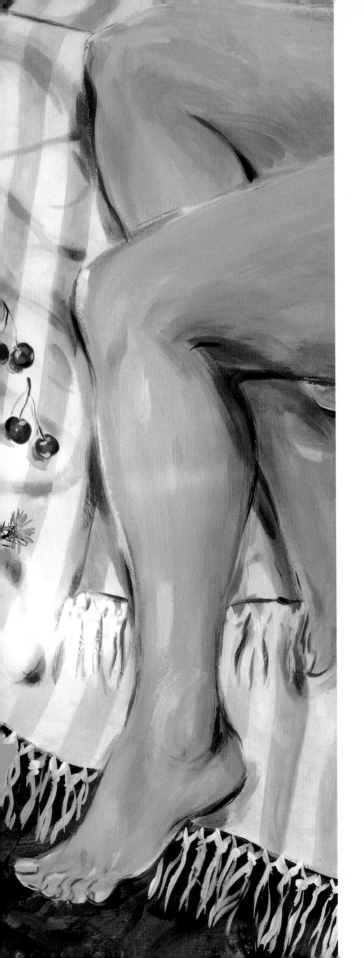

LÉGUMES
et
SALADES

*Whereas the average French
restaurant has a tendency
to dismiss vegetables as garniture,
a mere garnish, the home cook
traditionally uses them as
an important part of the meal.*

CAROTTES SAUTÉES

Sautéed Carrots with Cumin and Coriander

In France, vegetables are often served as starters, usually raw – or briefly blanched – to get the old gastric juices going. They then appear again as a side dish with the main meat or fish course. More often than not, there is a green salad to follow. Meat may be the luxury, the wonderful filling within the sandwich, but everybody knows that poor-quality bread can spoil a sandwich: the vegetable dishes that form the bulk of the meal are prepared simply but thoughtfully and are served one at a time in appetizing small amounts.

SERVES 4 • UNDER 25 MINUTES

400 g/14 oz young carrots, trimmed and scrubbed or peeled
½ garlic clove
1 tbsp olive oil
15-30 g/½-1 oz butter
¼ tsp ground cumin
¼ tsp ground coriander
few sprigs of parsley
sea salt and freshly ground black pepper

1 Bring a kettle of water to the boil. Leave baby carrots whole, but cut larger carrots on the slant into thickish slices.

2 Put the carrots in a large sauté pan. Cover generously with boiling water and season with salt. Return to the boil and blanch for 3-5 minutes over a high heat. Drain.

3 Rub the empty pan with the cut side of the garlic and return to a moderate heat.

4 Swirl in the oil, followed by the butter. Sprinkle in the cumin and coriander. Stir.

5 Add the carrots to the seasoned butter and stir to coat.

6 Reduce the heat, cover and cook gently for 10-15 minutes until tender, shaking the pan occasionally.

7 Snip in the parsley just before serving.

PETITS POIS À L'ÉTUVÉE

Stewed Baby Peas

Canned petits pois have got a sweet tenderness all of their own. The same recipe works well with baby frozen peas, but add a few tablespoons of light stock to the wilted lettuce and simmer until tender. Snip in spring onions and/or small strips of smoked or cured ham for a slightly stronger taste.

SERVES 4 • UNDER 15 MINUTES

several soft lettuce leaves
30 g/1 oz butter
400 g/14 oz canned petits pois
few sprigs of chervil
sea salt and freshly ground black pepper

1 Make a *chiffonnade* of the lettuce leaves. Tightly roll up each leaf and snip the roll across into fine shreds.

2 Melt half the butter in a wide saucepan over a low heat and add the lettuce shreds. Stir for 2 minutes until wilting.

3 Add the petits pois with their liquid and heat through gently, stirring occasionally.

4 Adjust the seasoning. Snip in a little chervil, stir again and serve with the juices.

COURGETTES À LA CRÈME

Creamed Courgettes

*Exactly the same method may be used to prepare leeks,
but first slice them into rings rather than sticks.*

SERVES 4 • UNDER 20 MINUTES

400 g/14 oz small firm courgettes
2 tsp oil
30 g/1 oz butter
1 generous tbsp crème fraîche, soured cream or
**   single cream**
few sprigs of tarragon
sea salt and freshly ground black pepper

1 Bring half a kettle of water to the boil.

2 Cut each courgette lengthwise into 4, then crosswise
into small sticks, no longer than 2 cm/¾ in.

3 Pour about 2.5 cm/1 in of the boiling water into a
sauté pan. Season with salt and bring back to a fast
simmer over a moderate heat.

4 Tip in the courgettes, bring back to a simmer and
cook for 2-3 minutes.

5 Drain well. Leave to cool a little in the colander, then
press dry with wads of paper towels – it does not matter
if you squash the courgette sticks in the process.

6 Return the pan to a moderate heat. Add the oil and
grease evenly with a wad of paper towels.

7 Tip in the courgettes and stir to dry for a minute.

8 Dot the butter around the pan, stir in and cook for a
minute.

9 Dribble in the cream and stir for a minute. Season to
taste, snip in the tarragon and serve.

HARICOTS VERTS AU PERSIL ET AUX PIGNONS

Parsleyed French Beans with Pine Nuts

SERVES 4 • UNDER 20 MINUTES

400 g/14 oz small French beans
1 tsp oil
15-30 g/½-1 oz butter
1 tbsp pine nuts or slivered almonds
several sprigs of parsley
sea salt and freshly ground black pepper

1 Bring a kettle of water to the boil. Top and tail the
beans a handful at a time, using scissors.

2 Put the beans in a sauté pan. Cover copiously with
the boiling water, season with salt and bring back to the
boil.

3 Cook over a high heat for 4-7 minutes, until almost
tender enough for your liking (the beans will go on
cooking a little after you drain them).

4 Drain well. Using a wad of paper towels, lightly
grease the empty pan with the oil. Return to a
moderate heat.

5 Swirl in the butter, then add the nuts and sauté for a
minute, stirring.

6 Tip the beans into the pan. Spread them evenly. Snip
in the parsley and stir for a minute. Season lightly and
serve immediately.

OVERLEAF
LEFT *Carottes Sautées*
RIGHT *Haricots Verts au Persil et aux Pignons*

ÉMINCÉ DE CHOU

Sautéed Cabbage Strips

SERVES 4 • UNDER 20 MINUTES

1 Savoy cabbage
2 juniper berries
1 scant tsp mixed peppercorns
1 tbsp oil
¼ tsp freshly grated nutmeg
30 g/1 oz butter
sprig of fresh thyme
sea salt and freshly ground black pepper

1 Bring a kettle of water to the boil.

2 Trim the cabbage, quarter it and cut out the hard core.

3 Put the cabbage quarters side by side in a wide heavy saucepan. Pour in enough of the boiling water to cover and season with salt. Bring to the boil over a high heat and continue simmering vigorously for about 3 minutes.

4 While the cabbage is cooking, coarsely crush together the juniper berries and peppercorns, using a pestle and mortar or a rolling pin.

5 When the cabbage is cooked, refresh it under cold running water and drain well. Leave until cool enough to handle.

6 Meanwhile, return the pan to a low heat and add the oil. When the oil is hot, add the crushed berries and the nutmeg to the pan. Stir for a minute. Add a small knob of butter, stir and keep over a low heat.

7 Squeeze the cabbage dry in a clean tea towel or between sheets of paper towel. Then cut it into thin shreds.

8 Turn the heat under the pan up to high. Add the shredded cabbage to the spice mixture, stir to coat and sauté for 2 minutes, stirring frequently.

9 Cover, reduce the heat a little and cook for 2-3 minutes, shaking the pan a few times.

10 Adjust the seasoning. Just before serving, rub the tiny thyme leaves off the stalk and stir into the cabbage with the rest of the butter.

FLAGEOLETS AUX OIGNONS ET TOMATES

Green Haricot Beans with Onion and Tomato

SERVES 4 • UNDER 15 MINUTES

1 tbsp olive oil
4 spring onions
170 g/6 oz canned chopped tomatoes, well drained
½ tsp dried thyme
450 g/1 lb canned flageolets, drained, rinsed and drained again
sea salt and freshly ground black pepper

1 Heat the oil in a wide saucepan. Snip in the spring onions, both white and green parts. Soften for 1 minute over a moderate heat.

2 Add the chopped tomatoes, season with a little dried thyme and salt and pepper. Cook for 3 minutes, stirring from time to time.

3 Tip in the flageolets and reduce the heat a little.

4 Heat through gently, adjust the seasoning and serve.

HARICOTS BLANCS AU BEURRE MAÎTRE D'HÔTEL

White Haricot Beans with Parsley Butter

We French are great believers in the honest but judicious use of cans, in moderation and usually with a little personal je ne sais quoi . . . Canned haricot beans, white haricots as well as pale green flageolets, are standard store-cupboard ingredients, as are canned petits pois and baby carrots (see the Introduction on page 13).

SERVES 4 • UNDER 15 MINUTES

55 g/2 oz soft butter
1 tsp lemon juice
several sprigs of parsley and a few chives
1 tbsp white wine
1 tsp oil
450 g/1 lb canned white haricot beans, drained, rinsed and drained again
sea salt and freshly ground black pepper

1 In a small cup, mash together the butter and lemon juice. Season generously with salt and pepper. Snip in plenty of fresh herbs.

2 Moisten a wide saucepan with the wine and oil. Add the beans and heat through over a very low heat.

3 Scatter the butter over the beans and fold in until melted.

FÈVES À L'ESTRAGON

Creamy Broad Beans with Tarragon

SERVES 4 • UNDER 15 MINUTES

350 g/12 oz frozen baby broad beans
15 g/½ oz butter
few sprigs of fresh tarragon or 1 tsp dried tarragon
1 generous tbsp crème fraîche or soured cream
sea salt and freshly ground black pepper

1 Bring a kettle of water to the boil.

2 Put the frozen broad beans in a sauté pan. Cover with the boiling water, season lightly and cook over a moderate heat for 5-7 minutes until just tender.

3 Drain well. Return the pan to a low heat, swirl in the butter and add the dried tarragon, if using. Tip in the broad beans and season lightly with salt and pepper.

4 Stir until well coated with butter. If using fresh tarragon, snip it in now and stir.

5 Dribble in the cream, stir again and serve immediately.

CHOUX DE BRUXELLES AU CARVI

Brussels Sprouts with Caraway

Some of my best friends hate them, but I have always had a penchant for sprouts, ever since I realized as a child that choux de bruxelles *could be enjoyed one by one like some sort of savoury bonbon. A well-cooked young sprout is a real treat – a little buttery on the outside, then a touch of crunch and a mellow centre with a unique flavour. I am, however, the first to agree that sprouts can be vile, if they are elderly or at all overcooked.*

SERVES 4 • UNDER 20 MINUTES

400 g/14 oz fresh top-quality sprouts, trimmed
1 tsp oil
15-30g/½-1 oz butter
1½ tsp caraway seeds
sea salt and freshly ground black pepper

1 Bring a kettle of water to the boil.

2 Put the sprouts in a large sauté pan. Cover generously with the boiling water and season with salt.

3 Boil over a moderate to high heat for 5-7 minutes until almost tender – keep checking after 4 minutes and on no account allow the sprouts to overcook.

4 Drain well. Pat dry with a wad of paper towels. Lightly oil the pan and place over a moderate heat.

5 Swirl in the butter and sprinkle in the caraway seeds. Stir until coated with butter.

6 Tip in the sprouts. Stir well into the caraway butter, season lightly and serve hot.

LEFT *Fèves à l'Estragon (page 99)*
RIGHT *Choux de Bruxelles au Carvi*

ÉPINARDS EN BRANCHE

Braised Leaf Spinach

So simple that I hesitate to spell it out as a recipe, this way with leaf spinach is a perfect accompaniment to a number of dishes, notably Steak Haché aux Anchois (see page 80) and Saint-Jacques Poêlées (see page 66).

SERVES 2 • UNDER 10 MINUTES

about 45 g/1½ oz butter
350 g/12 oz young leaf spinach, trimmed
small pinch of freshly grated nutmeg (optional)
sea salt

1 Melt half the butter in a sauté pan over a moderate heat.

2 Spread in the spinach, stir and cover.

3 Cook for 3 minutes, shaking the pan a few times.

4 Stir in the rest of the butter and a small pinch of nutmeg, if using. Season lightly with salt.

CHAMPIGNONS FARCIS

Stuffed Mushrooms

Butter with the oil is an optional extra – naturellement. A mild blue cheese or a fresh goats' cheese makes a nice alternative to cream cheese, but omit the anchovies. Serve with plain grilled steaks or chops, with bread and a mixed leaf salad as a main course for 2.

SERVES 4 • UNDER 30 MINUTES

12 medium unblemished brown-cap mushrooms
few drops of lemon juice
1 or 2 garlic cloves, chopped
few sprigs of flat leaf parsley
1 tsp dried thyme, or a mixture of savory and
marjoram
1 thick slice of slightly stale bread, crusts removed
2 canned anchovy fillets, drained and snipped
(optional)
85 g/3 oz light cream cheese
1 tbsp olive oil, plus extra for greasing and sprinkling
few drops of Tabasco sauce
dash of Worcestershire sauce
sea salt and freshly ground black pepper

1 Bring a kettle of water to the boil. Preheat the grill to high.

2 Put the mushrooms in a large pan. Cover with boiling water seasoned with a little salt and lemon juice. Return to the boil and simmer for a minute.

3 Drain and place on a double layer of paper towels. Pat dry and remove the stems (use for stock).

4 Generously oil a flameproof gratin dish.

5 In the food processor or small bowl, whizz or mash together the garlic, herbs, bread and anchovy, if using. Add the cream cheese and the tablespoon of oil. Season with salt and pepper, a few drops of Tabasco and Worcestershire sauce. Whizz again and adjust the seasoning if necessary.

6 Spoon a dollop of stuffing into each mushroom cap. Spread well with the back of the spoon or a palette knife. Sprinkle with a little extra olive oil.

7 Grill under a moderate heat for about 10 minutes, until bubbling hot. If necessary, turn the dish around to grill the mushrooms evenly. Serve hot or warm.

POIVRONS AU FOUR

Roasted Sweet Peppers

Charring peppers is a chore, so I always do more than I need at the time. Any leftovers will keep for a few days in the refrigerator. Add them to chopped avocado with a sprinkling of extra virgin olive oil and a teaspoon of lime or lemon juice for a light salad starter, or use up in a Piperade (see page 34).

SERVES 6 (4 ALLOWING FOR LEFTOVERS) • UNDER 45 MINUTES

3 large unblemished red peppers
2 large unblemished yellow peppers
1 large unblemished green pepper
2½ tbsp extra virgin olive oil
½-1 garlic clove, crushed
1 tsp finely grated zest from an unwaxed lemon or
    lime
sea salt and freshly ground black pepper

1 Preheat the oven to 230C/450F/gas8. Put the peppers side by side in a large roasting tin lined with a double layer of foil.

2 Roast for about 8 minutes, until the skins begin to blister. Turn over and bake for a further 5-7 minutes, until well charred. Remove from the oven, cover loosely with newspapers and leave to cool slightly.

3 When the peppers are cool enough to handle, peel off the skins. Pull out the core and seeds. Cut open the peppers and wipe the insides with paper towels to remove sticky seeds. Cut the peppers into long thin strips.

4 Collect the cooking juices from the foil.

5 Swirl the oil in a frying pan over a moderate heat. Dribble in the cooking juices and sprinkle in the garlic and grated zest. Stir.

6 Add the pepper strips to the pan and stir until hot. Season lightly and serve hot or warm.

POMMES POÊLÉES

Pan-fried Apples

A traditional companion for pork chops or black pudding pan-fried and finished with a little mustard and white wine reduction, this is also good with strips of duck breasts sautéed and glazed with a little port and redcurrant jelly.

SERVES 4 • UNDER 15 MINUTES

6 small crisp Cox's apples
1 tbsp oil
¼ tsp dried thyme
15 g/½ oz butter
sea salt and freshly ground black pepper

1 Quarter and core the apples.

2 Heat the oil in a frying pan until hot. Sprinkle in the thyme and swirl in half the butter.

3 Distribute the apples over the melted butter. Cover and cook over a low heat for 3 minutes, shaking the pan a few times.

4 Carefully turn the apples over. Dot the rest of the butter around the pan, turn up the heat a little and cook uncovered for 2-3 minutes. Season lightly and serve hot.

POMMES DE TERRE POÊLÉES

Sautéed Potatoes

These are a classic accompaniment to many dishes. They can also be the basis of satisfying main course dishes in themselves: sauté mushrooms in the frying pan while the potatoes are simmering, tip them out on two layers of paper towels, then add to the crispy potatoes just before serving. Grilled bacon, quickly boiled green beans and broccoli florets, a few spring onions or chopped tomatoes are other good additions to use in this way.

A glass of hearty Bergerac red will go down well with this easy potato-based supper.

SERVES 4 • UNDER 35 MINUTES

350 g/12 oz even-sized small, but not tiny, salad potatoes, well scrubbed
½ garlic clove
about 2½ tbsp olive oil
few sprigs each of parsley and chives
sea salt and freshly ground black pepper

1 Bring a kettle of water to the boil.

2 Put the potatoes in a wide saucepan or sauté pan and cover with the boiling water, allowing an extra 2.5 cm/1 in above them. Season with salt and return to the boil over a high heat.

3 As soon as the water bubbles, reduce the heat to a low boil. Cook the potatoes for about 12 minutes, until they are almost done but still a little too firm.

4 Drain well and refresh under cold running water. Leave to cool a little.

5 Rub the inside of a large frying pan with the cut side of the garlic. Heat half the oil in it until very hot.

6 Peel off the skins from the potatoes, then cut them into chunks. Season and spread in the pan.

7 Leave over a fairly high heat for 2 minutes without stirring to allow them to crisp and brown. Stir well, reduce the heat a little, sprinkle in some more oil and continue crisping and browning the potatoes for 2 minutes, shaking the pan occasionally.

8 Stir again, then sprinkle in the rest of the oil. Snip in the herbs and season lightly. Stir again and serve.

GRATIN DE POMMES DE TERRE EXPRESS

Quick Potato Gratin

Contrary to what you might think, potatoes cooked in fast-boiling water will not be ready sooner than potatoes cooked at a more modest simmer. The chances are they will turn out partly mushy, partly rock solid. For some reason, maybe because I am a stubborn Taurean, it took me a long time to accept this fact of life. My potato dishes are now much improved, thank you.

SERVES 4 • UNDER 35 MINUTES

350 g/12 oz even-sized small new potatoes, well scrubbed
about 2 tbsp olive oil, plus extra for greasing
½ tsp crushed dried thyme
¼ tsp dried marjoram or oregano
¼ tsp ground dried sage
15 g/½ oz butter, or more if preferred
sea salt and freshly ground black pepper

1 Bring a kettle of water to the boil.

2 Put the potatoes in a wide saucepan or sauté pan. Cover with the boiling water, allowing an extra 2.5 cm/1 in above them. Season with salt and return to the boil over a high heat.

3 As soon as the water bubbles, reduce the heat to a low boil. Cook the potatoes for about 15 minutes, until just done but still firm.

4 Preheat the grill to high. Oil a gratin dish or small baking sheet.

5 Drain the cooked potatoes and refresh under cold running water. Drain again and pat dry with paper towels.

6 Cut the potatoes into thickish slices and arrange them in the prepared dish or on the prepared baking sheet. Season generously with salt and pepper. Sprinkle with the dried herbs, then dribble over the oil and dot the butter over the top.

7 Grill until golden, shaking the dish and turning it a few times. Serve hot or warm.

Gratin de Pommes de Terre Express

PETITES PÂTES AUX ÉCHALOTES FONDUES

Pasta with Softened Shallots

Large amounts of pasta and noodles are consumed every day in France, but it would be dishonest of me to claim that they are authentic typical French fast fare. The fashion for main-course pasta is a recent one. However, small pasta, mini macaroni, coquillettes (literally little shells) and others have long been standard French side dishes.

A favourite way of serving pasta – and rice for that matter – as an accompaniment is to dress it with plenty of butter and grated Gruyère, with a sprinkling of parsley to finish. So good is this that it may even be served with a thick slice of cooked ham, jambon de Paris, followed by a green salad for a traditional homely supper à la française.

The following simple little recipe works very well with plain grills and sautés, leftover roast chicken or cold gigot of lamb. I also like it on its own as a starter with shavings of strong Gruyère or Parmesan.

SERVES 4 • UNDER 20 MINUTES

about 250 g/8½ oz dried pasta
1 tsp oil
200 g/7 oz fresh shallots (about 8 bulbs)
55 g/2 oz butter, plus a little extra if needed
sea salt and freshly ground black pepper

1 Bring a kettle of water to the boil. Put the pasta in a large pan and cover with the boiling water, allowing an extra 2.5 cm/1 in on top. Add a generous amount of salt and a trickle of oil and cook the pasta at a good rolling boil until tender but still firm to the bite.

2 Meanwhile, finely chop the shallots.

3 Melt the butter in a heavy saucepan over a low heat. Add the shallots and stir to coat with melted butter.

4 Cover and cook until soft over a low heat for 7-10 minutes, stirring the shallots a few times during cooking and shaking the pan from time to time. Add a little butter and take the pan off the heat for a few seconds if necessary. The shallots should soften, but not turn brown. Season lightly with salt and pepper.

5 Drain the pasta and toss with the shallots until well coated.

SALADE CHAUDE DE POMMES DE TERRE

Warm Potato Salad with Shallot Dressing

I find that the so-called 'salad' potatoes, sold in expensive little punnets on the posher vegetable shelves of supermarkets, simmer and peel much better than most other varieties. Their skin comes off in two or three movements, revealing smooth – almost glossy – flesh that does not break up easily . . . well worth the premium.

SERVES 4 • UNDER 30 MINUTES

450 g/1 lb even-sized small, but not tiny, salad potatoes, well scrubbed
1 shallot, finely chopped
½ garlic clove, crushed (optional)
3 tbsp olive oil
1 tbsp good-quality ready-made mayonnaise
several sprigs of flat leaf parsley
2 tsp red or white wine vinegar
sea salt and freshly ground black pepper

1 Bring a kettle of water to the boil.

2 Put the potatoes in a wide saucepan or sauté pan. Cover with the boiling water, allowing an extra 2.5 cm/ 1 in above them. Season with salt and return to the boil over a high heat.

3 As soon as the water bubbles, reduce the heat to a low boil. Cook the potatoes for about 15 minutes, until they are just done but still a little firm.

4 While the potatoes are cooking, make the dressing: in a small bowl, combine the shallot and garlic, if using, with the oil and mayonnaise. Snip in plenty of parsley. Whisk, add the vinegar, whisk again and season well.

5 Drain the potatoes and leave to cool a little. Pat dry with paper towels.

6 When the potatoes are cool enough to handle, peel off the skins. Then cut the potatoes into thick slices.

7 Tip half the potatoes into a serving bowl. Spoon over half the dressing and toss lightly until well coated. Add the rest of the potatoes and dressing and toss again.

8 Serve warm (tiède) or cold. The salad will keep well for a day or two in the refrigerator. Bring back to room temperature before eating.

PETITE PURÉE DE POMMES DE TERRE

Creamed Potatoes with Basil

This is perfect with slowly grilled Toulouse sausages or other plain meaty dishes and Flageolets aux Oignons et Tomates (see page 98) – or even good baked beans. The basil gives a distinctive flavour to the potatoes. If you prefer, use exactly the same method with flat leaf parsley, spinach or sorrel – or nothing at all if the potatoes are tasty enough. Thyme and chives also flavour the potatoes very nicely but they won't give so much of a green finish.

I was brought up using a bulky food mill, moulin à légumes, to make a light purée with its starch unbroken. I now have a ricer, which is fun to use and more convenient – unless you are making creamed potatoes for a crowd, which is a labour of love anyway.

SERVES 4 • UNDER 35 MINUTES

450 g/12 oz even-sized smallish firm salad potatoes, well scrubbed
45-55 g/1½-2 oz butter
4-6 basil leaves, or 1 scant tbsp pesto
3-4 tbsp milk
1 tbsp crème fraîche (optional)
sea salt and freshly ground black pepper

1 Bring a kettle of water to the boil.

2 Put the potatoes in a wide saucepan or sauté pan. Cover with the boiling water, allowing an extra 2.5 cm/ 1 in above them. Season with salt and return to the boil over a high heat.

3 As soon as the water bubbles, reduce the heat to a low boil. Cook the potatoes for about 15-17 minutes, until they are done but not soft. Drain well and refresh under cold running water. Leave to cool a little.

4 While they cool, put one-third of the butter in the pan and melt over a low heat. Snip in the basil and stir until soft or stir in the pesto. Add 3 tablespoons of milk.

5 Peel the skins off the potatoes, then lightly mash them. Whisk lightly to combine with the milk and basil butter. Add the rest of the milk – unless it looks too wet.

6 Still over a low heat, whisk in the rest of the butter, a knob at a time. Stir in the cream, if using, and adjust the seasoning. Serve hot.

LAITUE ET TRÉVISE AU JUS

Braised Lettuce with Radicchio

This somewhat tart and very simple braised salad is particularly good with fish and sautéed potatoes. Depending on what you serve it with, the amount of butter can vary.

SERVES 4 • UNDER 15 MINUTES

1 tsp oil
30-45 g/1-1½ oz butter
4 small lettuce hearts
4 small heads of radicchio, or several coarsely shredded leaves
pinch of freshly grated nutmeg
1 tsp soy sauce
sea salt and freshly ground black pepper

1 In a wide saucepan or sauté pan, combine the oil with half the butter. Heat over a moderate heat until the butter has melted.

2 Put in the lettuce and radicchio. Season with a little nutmeg, salt and pepper. Cover and cook for 3 minutes, shaking the pan occasionally.

3 Turn over the lettuce and radicchio. Dot with the rest of the butter and season again. Moisten with 2-3 tablespoons of water and sprinkle the soy sauce into the pan rather than on the lettuce and radicchio.

4 Cover and cook for another 3 minutes, shaking the pan several times. Serve moistened with the cooking liquid.

SALADE DE MÂCHE À LA BETTERAVE

Lamb's Lettuce and Beetroot Salad

Walnut kernels are an optional extra in this recipe. If, like me, you prefer your lamb's lettuce totally unadulterated, just toss it lightly with a little walnut oil mixed with groundnut oil. Season and chill for at least 20 minutes before eating.

SERVES 4 • UNDER 15 MINUTES

1 generous tbsp good-quality ready-made mayonnaise
1 tsp Dijon mustard
1 small baby beetroot, peeled and grated, or 1 equivalent piece of cooked beetroot cut into thin strips
100 g/3½ oz trimmed and washed lamb's lettuce
1½ tbsp olive oil, or 1 tbsp groundnut oil and 2 tsp walnut oil
1 tsp wine vinegar
sea salt and freshly ground black pepper

1 Combine the mayonnaise and the mustard in a bowl. Add the beetroot and toss to coat. Adjust the seasoning, if necessary.

2 In a serving bowl, toss together the lamb's lettuce, oil and vinegar. Season to taste.

3 Tip the dressed beetroot into the serving bowl. Toss lightly to combine it with the lamb's lettuce and serve immediately.

SALADE D'ENDIVES AUX NOIX

Belgian Chicory and Walnut Salad

This palate-cleansing salad can be made into a more substantial item by adding diced Gruyère and slivers of cooked, smoked or dry-cured ham.

SERVES 4 • UNDER 15 MINUTES

2 heads each of red and white Belgian chicory, cored and trimmed
2½ tbsp groundnut oil, plus extra for greasing
¼ tsp Dijon mustard
1 tsp red or white wine vinegar
1 tsp moist currants or small seedless raisins
¼ tsp sugar
2 tbsp fresh walnut kernels, quartered
sea salt and freshly ground black pepper

1 Separate the chicory heads into leaves and cut into attractive segments and pieces.

2 In a serving bowl, combine the oil with the mustard, vinegar, fruit and sugar. Season with salt and pepper.

3 Add the chicory to the bowl, toss until lightly coated and leave to stand for a few minutes.

4 Lightly grease a small frying pan and sauté the walnuts in it over a moderate heat for a minute or two. Season lightly.

5 Sprinkle the walnuts over the chicory, toss and serve.

PREVIOUS PAGES
LEFT *Salade d'Endives aux Noix*
RIGHT *Salade de Mâche à la Betterave*

SALADE PRINTANIÈRE

Mixed Leaf Spring Salad

SERVES 4 • UNDER 10 MINUTES

leaves from 1 head of soft lettuce
handful of rocket leaves, trimmed
small handful of baby spinach or sorrel leaves,
    trimmed and ribbed if necessary
several sprigs each of chervil and parsley
3 tbsp groundnut oil
2 scant tsp red wine vinegar
sea salt and freshly ground black pepper

1 Roughly tear the larger of the lettuce leaves. Mix well with the rocket and spinach in a suitable salad bowl.

2 Snip in the chervil and parsley. Mix again.

3 Combine the oil and vinegar in a small cup. Season generously with salt and sparingly with pepper.

4 Just before serving, dribble over the salad and toss lightly.

SALADE TIÈDE AUX TOMATES

Warm Tomato Salad

I sometimes sauté a few strips of anchovy and add them to the tomatoes in this dish and then finish with basil rather than mint. Either way it is good with Poussins Grillés au Citron Vert (see page 89), Saumon Poêlé au Poivre Vert (see page 76) and many other grilled or pan-fried fish dishes.

SERVES 4 • UNDER 15 MINUTES

about 12 small black olives, pitted
6-8 ripe firm tomatoes
¼ tsp dried savory, marjoram, thyme or oregano
2-3 tbsp extra virgin olive oil
1 tsp juice and ½ tsp finely grated zest from an
    unwaxed lemon
few leaves of mint or basil
sea salt and freshly ground black pepper

1 Bring a kettle of water to the boil.

2 Coarsely chop the olives.

3 Pour the boiling water into a large bowl. Drop in the tomatoes and leave for 1 minute.

4 Meanwhile, combine the chopped olives with the dried herbs, olive oil, lemon juice and zest in a small cup. Season to taste.

5 Drain and peel the tomatoes. Quarter and scoop out the seeds and some of the pulp. Tip the tomato quarters into a suitable serving dish.

6 Snip the mint or basil over the tomatoes. Dribble the olive and oil dressing on top, toss lightly and serve.

FROMAGES, FRUITS
et
DESSERTS

*For the French cook in a real hurry,
le dessert at weekday meals
tends to be cheese, yogurt or some
sort of fromage frais, followed
by fruit.*

COMPOTE D'ABRICOTS

Apricots in a Light Syrup

In France there are as many variations on the theme of compote de fruits maison as there are cooks with access to an orchard – or to a market in times of glut. This recipe also works well with peaches and nectarines. With plums, do not peel the fruit, simmer even more gently and shorten the cooking time a little. Whatever the fruit, serve it with small butter biscuits from Brittany and maybe a dollop of cream.

SERVES 4 • UNDER 20 MINUTES, PLUS CHILLING

450 g/1 lb firm ripe apricots
250 ml/8 fl oz white wine, or white wine mixed with
water, or just water
3 scant tbsp sugar
pinch of cinnamon
1 tbsp soft apricot jam
1 tbsp kirsch

1 Bring a kettle of water to the boil. Put the apricots in a saucepan, cover with the boiling water and simmer gently over a moderate heat for 2 or 3 minutes.

2 Meanwhile, in a separate saucepan bring to a simmer the wine, wine mixture or water with the sugar and cinnamon, stirring frequently.

3 Lift an apricot from the pan with a slotted spoon. With a small sharp knife, test that the skin peels off easily.

4 When they do, drain and peel the apricots, then cut in half and remove the stones.

5 Lower the apricots into the simmering syrup with the slotted spoon. Reduce the heat and poach for 3-4 minutes, depending on the fruit, until tender but not too soft.

6 Transfer the compote to a shallow cold (ideally chilled) serving bowl. Combine the jam and kirsch in a small jug or cup and stir lightly into the bowl. Allow to cool before serving or, better still, eat chilled.

POIRES AU ROQUEFORT

Poached Peaches with Blue Cheese Sauce

This dessert is designed for people who don't have a sweet tooth.

SERVES 4 • UNDER 30 MINUTES

4 firm but ripe Williams pears
300 ml/½ pt red wine mixed with 300 ml/½ pt water
3 tbsp sugar
15 g/½ oz unsalted butter
55 g/2 oz Roquefort or Fourme d'Ambert cheese
2 tsp brandy (optional)
1 tbsp cream cheese
1 tbsp Greek-style yogurt

1 Halve the pears, leaving the stalks attached. Pour the wine and water into a saucepan large enough to take the pear halves in a single layer. Stir in the sugar and bring to a simmer over a high heat, stirring a few times.

2 Meanwhile, core the pears, still trying to leave the stalks attached. Carefully shave off the peel, using a traditional peeling knife and not cutting into the flesh.

3 Lower the heat under the pan. Place the pears in the simmering liquid and poach them very gently for 5-10 minutes over a low heat, until they are tender but not squishy soft.

4 Using a slotted spoon, lift the pears from the pan and place them on paper towels. Leave to cool while making the cheese sauce.

5 Turn up the heat under the poaching liquid and simmer gently to reduce – do not allow to boil.

6 In a small heavy saucepan, melt the butter over a low heat. Crumble in the cheese and stir until melted. Stir in the brandy, if using, followed by the cream cheese and yogurt. Stir until smooth and heated through.

7 Arrange a pear on each of 4 dessert plates, with the two halves overlapping a little and at a slight angle. Moisten the pears with about 2 teaspoons of reduced poaching liquid. The rest can be gently reduced still more and used for another dessert recipe or – very sparingly – in a savoury sauce for duck or for venison sausages. Dribble the blue cheese sauce over the pears and serve immediately.

POMMES ET POIRES À LA POÊLE

Pan-fried Apples and Pears

This fry-up of a dessert is great on its own, particularly dressed with a soupçon of Calvados. For a proper treat, serve with one or more of the following: vanilla ice-cream, Greek-style yogurt and/or fromage frais with redcurrant jelly.

I sometimes use more or less the same method to sauté bananas. Cut 4 medium ripe but firm bananas in half lengthwise. Season with a touch of ground cinnamon and sauté as below, using half the amount of butter and sugar. Turn over after 3 minutes. Deglaze the pan juices with a generous tablespoon of rum or kirsch.

SERVES 4 • UNDER 25 MINUTES

4 small or 2 large firm ripe pears
4 small or 2 large eating apples
2 tsp lemon juice
85 g/3 oz unsalted butter
85 g/3 oz caster sugar
2 tsp Calvados or Poire Williams liqueur (optional)

1 Quarter, core and peel the pears. Quarter and peel the apples and sprinkle both with lemon juice.

2 Melt half the butter over a low heat in a large heavy frying pan. Sprinkle half the sugar as evenly as possible over the melted butter coating.

3 Place the pear wedges in the pan. Turn up the heat a little and sauté the pears for 3 minutes, shaking the pan a few times.

4 Add the apple wedges to the pan, pushing the pears aside to make room. Cook for 2 minutes as before.

5 Carefully turn over the pears and apples.

6 Cut the rest of the butter into small pieces and distribute in the pan between the pieces of fruit. Sprinkle with the rest of the sugar.

7 Turn up the heat. Cook for a further 5 minutes, until the pears and apples have turned a little golden and caramelized.

8 If you like, sprinkle with a little Calvados or Poire Williams liqueur. Serve hot or warm, perhaps with your choice of accompaniment(s) as above.

FROMAGES ET FRUITS

Fruit and Cheese

Fromage et fruit . . . the all-purpose everyday dessert. Note the order – cheese comes first in France. A 'proper' plateau de fromages consists of at least three different cheeses. For instance, try combining a ripe Camembert (its centre should bounce back a little when you press it), or a wedge of smooth even-coloured Brie, with a fresh goats' cheese and a piece of strong-tasting blue cheese. Unfortunately for cheese lovers, even in France, the average respectable plateau de fromages for a dinner party is likely to cost as much as the main course.

One solution is to make the cheese and fruit course a combined one. Stick to one cheese and go for top quality rather than variety. The following happy combinations are traditional:

• Camembert with the small crisp juicy apples of Normandy or Cox's Orange Pippins

• Comté or mature Gruyère with russet apples

• Brillat Savarin or other ultra-creamy cow's cheese with red grapes

• very fresh mild goats' cheese with white grapes

• Roquefort or Bleu d'Auvergne with ripe pears

BRIOCHES RÔTIES

Sweet Baked Brioche

This is good old-fashioned 'comfort food' and a very proper end for half a loaf of past-its-best brioche or sweet milky bread. As an alternative to the raspberry jam and almonds, try apricot jam and raisins moistened with kirsch.

SERVES 4 • UNDER 30 MINUTES

about 45 g/1½ oz soft unsalted butter, plus extra for greasing
4 thick slices of slightly stale brioche
2-3 tbsp soft raspberry jam
1 small egg
6 tbsp condensed or full-fat milk
about 3 tbsp caster sugar, or more if liked
pinch of ground cinnamon
3 tbsp slivered almonds

1 Preheat the oven to 200C/400F/gas6.

2 Generously butter a gratin dish and one side of each of the brioche slices.

3 Spread 2 generous teaspoons of jam over each buttered brioche slice. Put the brioche slices in the buttered dish, jam side up.

4 In a cup, whisk together the egg and milk. Whisk in 2 tablespoons of sugar and a pinch of cinnamon.

5 Spoon the egg mixture over the brioches.

6 Scatter the slivered almonds on top. Sprinkle with the rest of the sugar and dot with butter.

7 Bake for about 15 minutes until golden. Serve hot or warm.

BROCHETTES DE FRUITS CARAMÉLISÉES

Caramelized Fruit Kebabs

Very raffiné on the plate, these kebabs are full of pleasing contrasts on the palate. If you like, replace the fromage frais with some melted good-quality bitter chocolate: before grilling, brush with only half the amount of butter and sugar and omit the orange juice.

SERVES 2 • UNDER 20 MINUTES

mixture of ripe but firm fruit as available: such as apples, nectarines, grapes, clementines, pears, apricots, segments of fresh pineapple etc
45 g/1½ oz soft unsalted butter
3 tsp brandy or whisky
2 tsp juice and 1 tsp finely grated zest from an unwaxed orange
1 level tbsp cane sugar
1½ tbsp chilled fromage frais
1½ tbsp chilled Greek-style yogurt

1 Preheat the grill to high.

2 Cut the fruit into attractive segments. Thread very loosely lengthwise on 4 or 6 dampened wooden skewers.

3 In a small pan, heat the butter until melted. Combine with 2 teaspoons of the brandy or whisky, the orange juice and sugar.

4 Brush the flavoured butter over the fruit.

5 Grill under a moderate heat for 1-2 minutes each side, turning over the kebabs once.

6 Whisk the fromage frais with the yogurt until combined. Stir in the rest of the brandy or whisky and the orange zest.

7 Arrange 2 or 3 fruit skewers on each plate. Dribble over any pan juices and spoon half the flavoured fromage frais on the side.

RIGHT *Brochettes de Fruits Caramélisées*
OVERLEAF
LEFT *Pêches au Vin (page 122)*
RIGHT *Coupe de Fruits d'Été (page 122)*

COUPE DE FRUITS D'ÉTÉ

Summer Fruit Salad

This fruit combination is one that I enjoy, but do adapt it to suit your taste and the fruit available. What is nice about this simple dessert is that the fruit looks at the same time irresistibly fresh and easy to eat.

Spend a few minutes preparing the fruit platter before the meal and chill while you eat the first courses. Peel the fruit, if necessary, and cut the larger ones into wedges and slices. Arrange these in loose concentric circles to look more like a fruit tart topping than a conventional fruit salad.

SERVES 4 • UNDER 15 MINUTES, PLUS CHILLING

**1 white peach
1 nectarine or 1 yellow peach
2 apples
1 pear
2 large plums
2 heaped tbsp fraises des bois or small ripe
    strawberries
2 heaped tbsp raspberries
3 tbsp freshly squeezed orange juice
1½ tbsp Cointreau, plus extra to serve
juice of 1 lime and finely grated zest of ½ lime
icing sugar to taste (optional)**

1 Bring a kettle of water to the boil. Put the peach and nectarine in a saucepan, cover with the boiling water and bring back to the boil.

2 Leave to bubble gently for a minute or two over a moderate heat. Lift out of the water with a slotted spoon and peel when cool enough to handle.

3 Cut all the large fruit into attractive wedges. Arrange these with the berries on a large platter or coupe.

4 In a small jug, combine the orange juice, Cointreau and lime juice, reserving one or teaspoons of lime juice. Sweeten with a little icing sugar.

5 Dribble the mixture over the salad and chill while eating the rest of the meal.

6 Just before serving, accentuate the flavours with a few extra drops of Cointreau and lime juice. If you like, dredge lightly with a sifting of icing sugar.

PÊCHES AU VIN

Peaches in Wine

When there is more time, for slightly special occasions or for the benefit of senior relatives, children and sweet-toothed members of the family, there will be a simple sweet, often fruit-based. Nothing very elaborate, since the time and effort go into the rest of the meal. For a plate of exquisite petits fours the French rely on the skills of the local pâtissier. However, every home cook in France, even the most reluctant, has a small repertoire of favourite quick desserts.

Fruit with wine or alcohol makes a convenient quick dessert. If you are too pushed for time to prepare your peaches before the meal, serve them en famille-style: i.e. don't peel the peaches and put all the ingredients on the table for a d.i.y. dessert.

SERVES 4 • UNDER 15 MINUTES, PLUS CHILLING

**4 ripe peaches
icing sugar to taste
500 ml/16 fl oz medium or dry chilled rosé or white
    wine, preferably sparkling
few sprigs of mint, to decorate
small fresh macaroons, to serve**

1 Bring a kettle of water to the boil.

2 Put the peaches side by side in a saucepan. Cover with the boiling water and bring back to the boil. Leave to bubble gently for a minute or two over a moderate heat.

3 Lift the peaches out of the pan with a slotted spoon. Peel off the skin. Cut them in half and remove the stone.

4 Put each peach together again and place in a glass or coupe. Sweeten to taste with a dredging of icing sugar, using a small fine sieve. Cover with wine and chill while eating the preceding courses.

5 Put a small sprig of mint in each glass and serve with a few small macaroons.

PETITES MOUSSES AU CHOCOLAT

Chocolate Pots

Yes, the good news is that chocolate mousse can be lightly set in just about 30 minutes, if you use small chilled ramekins as follows.

SERVES 4 • UNDER 20 MINUTES, PLUS 30 MINUTES CHILLING

115 g/4 oz top-quality dark bitter chocolate
2 tbsp Cointreau
45 g/1½ oz soft unsalted butter
2 very fresh large eggs, separated
3 scant tbsp caster sugar
2 generous tbsp full-fat mild cream cheese or double cream

1 Turn the refrigerator to the highest setting and chill 4 small ramekins on the coldest shelf while preparing the mousse.

2 Break the chocolate into small pieces, straight into a heavy saucepan. Add the Cointreau and butter. Warm over a very low heat until melted and smooth, stirring very frequently with a wooden spoon.

3 Meanwhile, in a bowl, beat together the egg yolks and the sugar until pale and thickened.

4 Take the pan off the heat and stir in the yolk mixture, working briskly until completely combined.

5 Quickly stir in the cream cheese or cream until totally absorbed. Leave to cool on a cold surface, stirring once or twice.

6 Whisk one of the egg whites until just stiff (keep the other for another recipe). Using a metal spoon or a small whisk, fold a spoonful of beaten egg white into the chocolate. Fold in the rest, working quickly with light upward movements until there are no white streaks left in the mixture.

7 Spoon into the ramekins. Chill in the coldest part of the refrigerator for 30 minutes or until ready to eat.

8 To serve as a little party piece: put each ramekin and a shiny teaspoon on a pretty plate with 3 fanned-out langues de chat. Pile a small mound of berries on the plate and dust lightly with icing sugar. Spoon a dollop of yogurt at the end opposite the biscuits.

TATIN EXPRESS

Quick Upside-down Apple Tart

A favourite family shortcut . . . you can bake this when it is most convenient for you and finish it off under the grill just before eating – the tart itself does not have to be piping hot when served.

SERVES 4-6 • UNDER 45 MINUTES

100 g/3½ oz soft unsalted butter, plus extra to finish
115 g/4 oz caster sugar, plus extra to finish
675 g/1½ lb small crisp eating apples
225 g/½ lb chilled sheet of ready-made shortcrust pastry
Petite Crème (see page 17) or good vanilla ice-cream, to serve

1 Preheat the oven and a large baking sheet to 200C/400F/gas6.

2 Generously butter the base and sides of a large loose-bottomed tart tin, reserving about 30 g/1 oz butter. Sprinkle the tin generously and evenly with sugar, reserving 1 or 2 tablespoons.

3 Quarter and core the apples. Then arrange them tightly in the prepared tin. Dot with the rest of the butter and sprinkle with the rest of the sugar.

4 Put the pastry sheet over the apples. Trim it to fit the tin and tuck it in well all round between the apples and the tin.

5 Bake on the hot baking sheet for about 25 minutes, until the pastry is cooked. Check after 15 minutes and reduce the heat if the pastry is browning too fast. Leave to cool for a few minutes.

6 Preheat the grill to high. Protecting your hands with oven gloves, invert the tin on a flameproof serving dish. Remove the ring and base – you may need to re-arrange the apple topping a little.

7 Dot a little extra butter over the apples, sprinkle lightly with sugar and grill until brown and bubbly. Serve warm with Petite Crème or vanilla ice-cream.

TARTELETTES AUX FRUITS MAISON

Quick Fruit Tartlets

These can be topped with a single type of fruit or a mixture. Put them in the oven when you sit down to eat and they will bake during the course of the meal.

SERVES 4 • UNDER 45 MINUTES

24 cm/9½ in square of chilled ready-rolled puff pastry
1 tbsp milk
about 15 g/½ oz butter for greasing
flour, for dusting
Petite Crème (page 17), to serve

FOR THE TOPPING
about 6 generous tbsp redcurrant jelly, apricot or
raspberry jam or orange marmalade
firm ripe prepared fruit: such as orange segments,
grapes, apricot wedges, strawberries and
raspberries and plum wedges

1 Preheat the oven to 220C/425F/gas7. Grease a baking sheet generously with butter and dust it with flour.

2 Using a large biscuit cutter, cut out four 10 cm/4 in circles from the chilled pastry. Place the circles on the prepared baking sheet. Turn up the edge of each circle to make a rim and slit with a knife at regular intervals. Brush the rim with a little milk.

3 Make the topping: in a small saucepan, very gently heat the jelly, jam or marmalade until runny and syrupy. Brush most of this glaze lightly over the pastry base, but avoiding the rim. Arrange the fruit evenly and attractively on top of the syrupy glaze. Brush a little more glaze over the fruit.

4 Bake the tarts for 20-25 minutes, until the pastry is cooked through. Check after 15 minutes: if the topping is browning too fast, cover loosely with crushed foil.

5 Using a spatula, check that the pastry bases are crisp enough before removing from the oven. Reheat the remaining glaze and brush it lightly on top of the tarts. Serve warm, rather than hot, with the cream.

LEFT *Tarte Tatin (page 123)*
RIGHT *Tartelettes aux Fruits Maison*

INDEX

ACKNOWLEDGEMENTS

The Author would like to give a big thank you to the entire team who worked on the book. For their inspiration, wit, tasting comments and helpful criticisms she would also like to express her gratitude to many people: in particular, Lewis Esson, Henrietta Green, Colin MacIvor, Françoise Moine and Pierre-André Touttain.

The Publishers would like to thank Tom's, 225 Westbourne Grove, London W11 for their help in supplying props for photography.